ROCK CLIMBING

ROCK CLIMBING

by

Stan Wroe

First published 1979 by Oxford Illustrated Press

Printed and bound by Butler and Tanner Ltd, Frome, for Oxford Illustrated Press Ltd, Shelley Close, Headington, Oxford

ISBN 0 902280 61 9

Contents

	page number
Introduction	9
Some Climbing Terms and Climbers' Knots	16
Modern Climbing Practice	21
Equipment	27
Free Climbing Techniques	47
Protection Techniques	56
Descent Technique: Abseiling	66
Self Rescue: Prusiking	74
Guide Books and Grading	77
Equipment Check List	82
Climbing Areas and Associations	84
UK Climbing Clubs	87

Foreword

I believe there's no finer sport than rock climbing, and today young people are taking it up as never before. For some, it represents a breakaway from jobs and everyday lives which offer little personal challenge; others become so keen that they uproot themselves from the cities so that they can live close to the mountains. And it's not only the young who can find enjoyment by rock climbing, there are many people of middle years and older who climb most weekends; their experience more than makes up for what they might have lost in strength. Physique is less important than in other sports, good climbers come in all shapes and sizes. It is a sport which girls can become good at, climbing with rhythm and balance rather than brute force.

In terms of climbing technique, there are some important items which are rarely mentioned. The most important is the development of a sound judgement of your own abilities; be alert to danger at all times and if the warning bells sound in your head, back off and think again. It is no disgrace to fail to climb a route—you can always try it another day. Another factor is the ability to rest in difficult situations; rock climbing, with its many short explosive bursts of effort, can be very tiring on arms and fingers. Conserve your strength by keeping your hands low, thus maintaining a steady blood supply to them. Wherever you can, keep the whole of your weight on your feet. This is often possible by using small footholds to rest, which might in themselves offer nothing in the way of further progress. Bridging techniques can be used in this way. Mental control is an important point which is not often considered in a positive way. There is a natural tendency to panic when in a frightening situation, and all rock climbers experience this at some time. Panic is completely counter productive, since the person gripped by it is not capable of effective action to remedy the situation. Learn to control it and you will benefit greatly.

When you first begin to climb, you will be seconding all the time; remember that leading is a more rewarding experience and paradoxically, the climbing often seems easier. The beginner should be encouraged to lead easy pitches early in his career.

Modern methods of protection, together with advanced equipment, has made rock climbing a much safer sport than it was a few years ago; learn to use your gear with competence, and have due regard for the ethics of your sport. Good climbing!

Joe Brown

Introduction

Rock climbing is a most important skill within the greater sport of mountaineering, but it has become a very popular adventure sport in its own right, all over the world. Indeed, many rock climbers spend their time on outcrops and sea cliffs, and might never attempt a mountaineering route at all.

During the Victorian era of prosperity spawned by the Industrial Revolution, the wealthy English started the fashion for mountaineering in the Western Alps, and with local men as guides made the first ascents of many major peaks. Men such as Whymper and Mummery were pre-eminent amongst the early mountaineers. During the Alpine off season, it became usual for gentlemen climbers to visit the Lake District or Snowdonia two or three times a year in order to rock climb to keep in practice. From these beginnings the sport of rock climbing began for its own sake. The earliest climbs were made in gullies or chimneys, since these offered the easiest lines; eventually the climbers pushed out on to the bolder face routes. Now, with improved equipment and protection techniques it sometimes seems as if every nook and cranny of every cliff must have been climbed, yet new climbs, even new cliffs, continue to be found. What is it then, that makes rock climbing such an attractive sport?

It's not easy to explain, and certainly many climbers make no attempt to analyse their own feelings about it. Essentially the attraction is twofold: there is the physical pleasure of movement up great rock faces in sunshine and shadow, but much more important is the mental struggle between the desire for success and the fear of falling. This means total absorption in the climb, and the kind of mental concentration required in a difficult game of chess.

Since rock climbs are given a grading, it is possible for the climber to pick routes near the upper limit of his ability. He is thus continually tested both mentally and physically. But even if he has the best of physiques and the courage of a lion, without a sound sense of judgement of his

Opposite *Because it is there? This pair have climbed the little pinnacle in the Vajolet Towers and are preparing to abseil off.*

Right *An Alpine grade V route: Papillons ridge, Aiguille du Peigne, Mont Blanc. Like many routes on the Chamonix aiguilles it is a pure rock climb, without snow or ice. Climbs are often started from a mountain hut or, as this one, from a high camp. If you intend to use Alpine huts often you would do well to join the Austrian Alpine club, which enables large savings on hut fees. They have a British section.*

own capabilities, a climber will soon find himself in trouble. A leader's brain is an involved computer, assessing balance, friction, protection, and his own muscular fatigue. He must learn by experience to look at the next twenty, or two hundred, feet of his route, and make his own judgements about the possible dangers in store.

There are other obvious attractions; the climber often finds himself in beautiful places, perhaps in the mountains, but also climbing on sea cliffs or moorland tors. Many climbers travel abroad to climb. How much better to travel with a definite and difficult purpose in mind, rather than the aimlessness of lolling on a beach!

For those who live in Britain there is a wealth of rock climbing, and it's as well to remember that, like so many other sports, the British started it all, though it's true that home rock climbing was regarded as practice for the sterner stuff abroad.

Unless you live in East Anglia, there will be some climbing within an hour's journey or so from your home. Kent has its sandstone outcrops, Sussex and Dorset their sea cliffs, Devon its tors, and so on; all over the country can be found rock climbing on sea cliffs and quarries, mountain crag and outcrop.

There are many different types of rock; and each gives its own style of climbing. The younger granites have large slabs and faces with deep parallel cracks, the older igneous rocks such as

One of the short, fierce, problem climbs, Neb Direct at Tremadoc, graded Extreme E4. The climber is Paul Trower (photo: Dave Lancely).

Rock varies greatly in quality and texture. This is the compacted shale of Tintagel Head in Cornwall, and the climb is one of the great modern routes, 'Il Duce', Extreme E3. The climber here, John Eastham, is the middle man in a rope of three (photo: Rob Matheson).

Clogwyn D'ur Arddu, the 'black cliff of the black height', the finest cliff south of the Scottish Highlands. The climber is on the left-hand variant of Bow Shaped Slab, graded Hard VS.

The Dolomites are a wonderful area for the rock climber, and enjoy much better weather than the French Alps. (This is also true of the northern Tyrolean ranges of the Kaisergebirge, and the Karwendel.) For anyone with a limited summer holiday, with no time to wait for climbs in the Western Alps to come into condition, and with the modern super highways, it takes only an easy 24 hours' drive from Ostend.

Gritstone quarry climbing at Heptonstall in Lancashire. The graffiti visible at the top are just one of the penalties of climbing in an urban environment.

porphyry and dolerite have many more incut holds, and the routes tend to be more complex. The sedimentary rocks such as gritstone are characterized by rough texture which offers good friction, but the naturally occurring outcrops (as opposed to quarries), often have rounded holds caused by wind erosion. Limestone climbing, which has become popular in recent years, is sometimes steep and often loose.

Most climbers will spend one or two evenings a week in summer climbing on local outcrops, and will often travel overnight at weekends to reach the longer climbs to be found in Wales, the Lake District or Scotland. Bank holidays are the times of trips to more distant venues such as Cornwall, or perhaps Arran. Long summer holidays are reserved for visits to the more remote parts of Britain, northern Scotland, Donegal or Lundy Island, which are just a few of the possibilities. However, for the really big rock climbs, it is necessary to travel abroad where the prospects are endless. The fairytale spires of the Dolomites offer climbs of all grades of difficulty, up to 4000 feet in length; the great North West Wall of the Civetta is over three miles long, and averages 2500 feet in height, with many difficult routes for the accomplished climber. In the Western Alps, the Chamonix Aiguilles are the Mecca of the British climber, and a large contingent are to be found there every summer. Of course, where a big rock climb involves the ascent of mountains over around 8000 feet in height, a fair amount of mountaineering knowledge will be required; by this we mean the ability to interpret weather patterns, to find the route in difficult conditions, and to move quickly for long periods.

Some of the greatest rock climbs in Europe finish on the summits of high mountains, and climbers who intend to try these should have a reasonable knowledge of both ice climbing techniques and mountain navigation—particularly for making a safe descent.

Rock climbing is an adventure sport, and adventure implies risk, there can be no denying the fact. Yet the number of climbers injured while climbing is a minute proportion of the number of participants. Safety techniques are so well-developed that injuries are rare, and modern hard climbs so steep that a falling climber won't hit the rock. Many reported 'climbing' accidents occur to fell walkers rather than rock climbers, but indifferent news media lay the blame at the door of the climber.

What are the age limitations for rock climbing? Really there are none, though I would only take a beginner under the age of, say, fourteen in the middle of a rope of three where he would have little responsibility. At the older end of the scale, providing a person feels fit, there is absolutely no reason why he or she shouldn't climb until well past sixty.

There are various ways of beginning to climb. A popular way for children of school age is to take a course at an outdoor pursuits centre. These are usually run by education authorities, many of which own centres in mountainous country, and employ professional instructors. Courses are for one or two weeks, and take place all through the year. Grants are available to children whose parents are of limited means.

Another good way to begin is to join a climbing club. A list of these is given on pages 87–92. Here you will find people keen to give you a good start, and you will certainly find someone who will take you climbing in safety for those first few important occasions. Another problem which a club will solve is transport; climbers are great travellers, and are always ready to help with a lift at weekends and for longer holidays. Club members will probably lend, or even give,

The great discovery of the sixties, Craig Gogarth, which falls straight into the Irish Sea from the summit of Holyhead Mountain. There are now two hundred fine climbs on this cliff and its twin, South Stack. The climbers here are on Diogenes Hard VS.

equipment to get a young person started, which is an important point considering the cost of gear.

It is by no means impossible to start to climb by your own effort. If there is a local crag with which you're familiar, a visit to it will probably reveal someone in like mind to yourself. However, under no circumstances should you start climbing alone, or solo, as climbers say; without experience you are asking for trouble.

Whatever you do, it's a good idea to join the British Mountaineering Council, which effectively represents all climbers' interests. They need your financial and your vocal support for their efforts to maintain access to crags on private property, and to ward off sometimes over-zealous environmentalist groups.

Opposite *Creation, a recent E4 climb on Raven Crag, Thirlmere, in the Lake District. The climber, Ron Fawcett, is laying away on an undercling before stepping up to the right edge. A protection peg is below his left foot (photo: Rob Matheson).*

Above right *In Britain most rock climbers travel at weekends to areas such as the Lake District, Glencoe or Cornwall. Here, in Snowdonia, the vast majority camp in tents. However, there are quite a number of climbing huts owned by clubs, offering good accommodation at low prices. Often, clubs will have reciprocal arrangements with other clubs for hut use and so it is not necessary always to climb in the same area. This hut is Ynws Ettws, owned by the Climbers' Club, and is in the Llanberis Pass.*

Below *Reminiscent of Chamonix granite, this is in fact the Rosa Pinnacle of Chir Mhor on the Isle of Arran. The direct route takes the S-shaped crack prominent in the upper face, and gives a pleasant climb of close on a thousand feet at about Mild VS standard. If you sail across in a dinghy, taking camping gear, a memorable week can be guaranteed.*

Climbing Terminology

Before reading the chapters on technique and equipment, it will help if the reader is familiar with some of the terms in common usage.

Abseil Descent by sliding down a doubled rope using a friction brake. Very commonly used by climbers. The French word *rappel* is sometimes used.

Aid The momentary use of artificial aids such as pegs, skyhooks or nutslings when free climbing. Use of aid is acceptable only when stated in the route description.

Arête Ridge.

Artificial Climbing Use of equipment such as pegs or bolts to overcome long sections of a climb which would be impossible by other means, for instance horizontal overhangs.

Belay Anchor point on the rock face, being the position where a climber can secure himself to the rock and, by placing the ropes around his body (or using one of the other methods), can safeguard the rest of the party. See chapter on Protection Techniques, page 56.

Belay Chain The whole belay arrangement considered as one unit, i.e. the point of attachment, its sling, the belayer's harness, the belay method, main ropes, running belays, and the karabiners used.

Bight The loop formed by doubling a rope.

Bouldering The various climbing techniques are often practised on large fallen boulders or small cliffs. There are some popular boulder climbs of such technical difficulty that they rate as climbs in their own right. It is usual to solo boulders.

Chimney Wide crack in the rock, big enough to admit the climber's body.

Clean Climbing Leaving the rock as you find it, undamaged by pegs, and unmarked by chalk.

Knots

Two important climber's knots: the Figure 8 (left) and the bowline (right). Since nylon rope is slippery and flexible, it is usual to secure further any knots made with a half hitch.

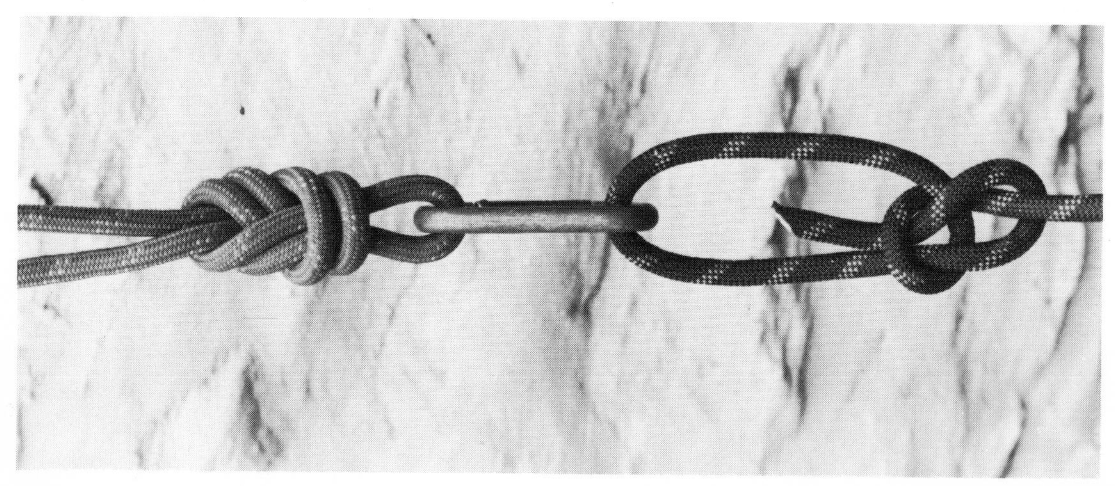

Crux A very difficult section of a climb, involving a single move only, or several moves in succession. A climb might have more than one crux.
Dièdre Corner formed by two rock walls (*dihedral* in the United States).
Exposure In a climbing sense, exposure implies an airy situation with a potential long drop were the climber to fall.
Fall Factor The length of a fall divided by the length of rope run out. It is expressed in decimals and can vary between 0 and 2.
Free Climbing The usual practice of modern climbing, where no aid is used.
Gully Steep defile in a rock face, which is often wet.
Grade The degree of difficulty of a climb is denoted by its grade. Many different grading systems are in use in the world. See chapter on Grading, page 77.
Grip In climber's vernacular, a frightening experience.
Groove A long, shallow depression in the rock face.
Impact Force The maximum force which a rope (i.e. the climber too!) will have to absorb during a fall. Ropes with low stretch generate high impact forces and vice versa.

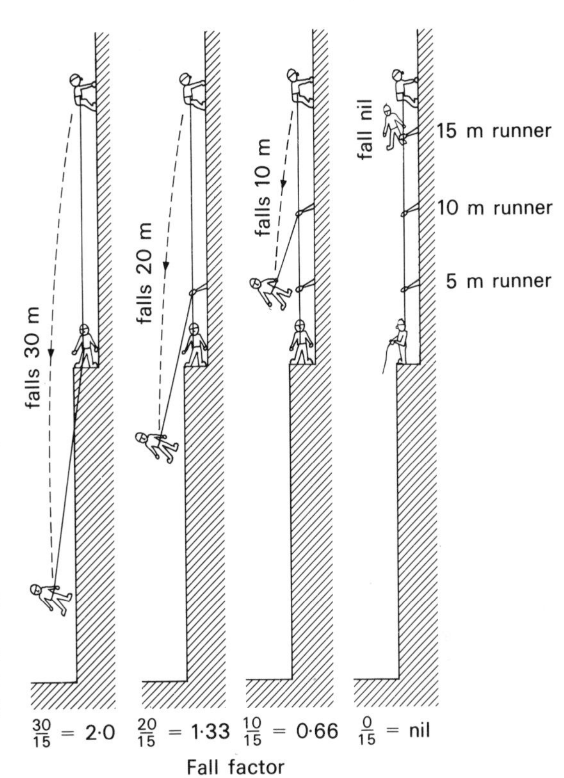

Fall Factor *This is defined as the distance a climber falls, divided by the amount of rope run out from the belay. A leader without any runners on experiences a fall of factor 2, the most severe of any fall. It is interesting to note that if he has a runner near to him when he falls, he experiences a softer fall when he is high above his second than when he is nearer to him.*

Left *Tape knot. An overhand knot is made in one tape and its partner is threaded through and round it in the opposite direction. As this knot is also inclined to work loose, the tape ends should be stitched, or otherwise held fast, by electrical tape.*

Right *Prusik knot. Reliable and effective and with several variants, it can be tied with one hand. It becomes difficult to move when the ropes are wet, however; the Bachmann knot is better in this circumstance.*

The double fisherman's knot used for joining two ropes, or the ends of a sling. Here it is shown loose (left) and tightened (right).

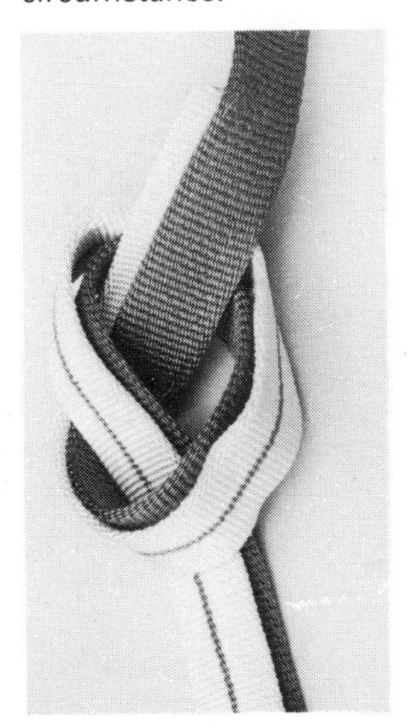

Karabiner An oval piece of steel or alloy, rather like a chain link. It has a gate in one side so that ropes can be easily clipped in. The karabiner has many uses in rock climbing.
Kernmantel Modern climbing rope, made from synthetic materials and having a core of parallel fibres contained in a braided sheath.
Leader The first man of a party to climb a pitch. His is the greatest risk, since he has no rope above him as a safeguard, and the greatest responsibility. His position is often referred to as 'the sharp end'.
Line The route which a rock climb takes.
Main Ropes The ropes used as a lifeline when climbing; one or two ropes might be used depending on preference; two ropes are more usual in Britain and Europe.
Normsturze The number of falls sustained by a rope before breaking, when tested by the standard UIAA test.
Party The group of climbers joined by the same rope; sometimes referred to as the 'rope', and occasionally as the 'team'. This is usually two people in modern climbing practice.
Peg Metal spike driven into the rock for use as a belay.
Pitch The stretch of rock climbing between two belay points. The length of a pitch will be determined by such factors as the availability of belays, or the length of the ropes in use.
Protection In climbing parlance, protection refers to running belays placed by the leader as he climbs a pitch. Where many runners are attached, the climb is said to be well protected. A leader who places a lot of protection is said to have 'stitched' the pitch. The quantity of slings which every climber carries, are referred to collectively as his 'protection'.
Prusik To climb the main ropes using special knots or mechanical devices. See page 74.

The Munter, or Italian, hitch. It is a sliding hitch which causes friction as the rope runs across itself. It is really half a clove hitch as its German name halbmastwurf *indicates.*

A useful variant on the prusik knot is the Bachmann knot. The karabiner provides a good handhold, while making the knot less likely to jam than the ordinary prusik knot.

Runners or **Running Belays**, i.e. as opposed to fixed belays. These are slings attached to the rock as the leader climbs a pitch. By means of a karabiner, his ropes are attached to the runner which is intended to limit a possible fall. Up to twenty might be used on a pitch.
Route The climb.
Second Any member of the climbing party who is not leading.
Scree Rocky detritus piled below a crag.
Slab A rock face up to about seventy degrees in angle; steeper than this it becomes a wall.
Skyhook Metal hook used for aid.

Solo Climbing Climbing alone. It can involve a number of specialized techniques.

Stance A ledge big enough to stand on. It is usually associated with a belay.

Stumblebum One who kicks rocks down on others.

Tension Rope technique where the leader is able to use tension from the main ropes as aid.

UIAA Union Internationale des Associations d'Alpinisme. An international body chiefly concerned with the improvement of safety standards in mountaineering.

Chocks are no good on this pitch—let's try the tranquillisers

The Vajolet Towers in the Catnaccio area of the Dolomites. The Dolomites offer splendid climbing on their limestone spires. The route up the left arête is very popular and, though steep and exposed, is only graded IV, about Severe by British standards.

Modern Climbing Practice

Rock climbs are made on mountain crags, sea cliffs, outcrops or, in their greatest form, on major mountains. A climb follows natural lines of weakness in the rock; often gullies, chimneys or cracks. After the first ascent of a climb, the route is given a name and a grade, usually by the first ascent party, and the details are published in the appropriate guide book for the area. This applies to rock climbs great and small throughout the world, from Harrison's rocks in Kent to the great faces of the Dolomites.

A route is divided into pitches, the length of each of these being determined by the availability of naturally occurring stances. A pitch might vary between 20 feet and 165 feet, which is the maximum length of rope used. Many outcrop climbs are one-pitch routes, while at the other extreme some of the longer mountain routes can have over forty pitches. Ideally, a climb should not be crossed by another, easier route since this detracts from the purity of line, but in practice it is not uncommon for different climbs to share stances or even pitches.

The Team

A climbing party usually consists of two people, sometimes three. Four climbers rarely climb on one rope except in unusual circumstances because of the delays involved (one man climbing, three waiting); it is generally more satisfactory to split the party into two ropes of two.

The first man who climbs a pitch, taking up the rope to protect the others is the 'leader', and the rest of the party, however many, are 'seconds'. The leader has no rope directly above him to prevent him from falling, and he is therefore in a position of danger and responsibility. It follows that the leader should be the most experienced climber in the party; the more so since he will have the responsibility of routefinding as the climb progresses. It is quite usual with two experienced climbers for each to lead alternate pitches; by doing this time is saved, since there is no need to change belays. It is also more satisfying if each has the responsibility and interest of leading in turn; often it works out that

Climbs follow natural features as with this leftward sloping crack on Craig Gogarth. The leader will assess the protection required as he moves up, and will look for a resting place before attempting the crux of the climb (the moves round the arête thirty feet above him). This climb is Strike, Extremely Severe E3; the pitch is graded 6a.

A one-pitch climb; the leader has run out about a hundred feet of rope. In another twenty feet he will reach a belay position on a ledge, using the small trees as anchors. He will then take in any slack rope and bring up his second by taking in the ropes as the second climbs. In this way the second is continually safe-guarded.

one climber will prefer to lead crack pitches, and the other slabs.

Climbing Sequence

In a party of two, the leader climbs the first pitch, putting on runners for protection as need or sense dictate; his main ropes are paid out as he climbs by his second, who is secured to the rock, i.e. belayed. If the leader should fall, his highest runner will hold him; the main ropes held by his second will be subjected to a strong upwards pull, and the second must be belayed in such a manner as to resist this. The methods of arresting the fall will be dealt with in the chapter on belaying, but they are all dependent on the second holding the rope tightly in order to apply a controlled braking force.

When the leader has succeeded in climbing the pitch (i.e. has reached a stance), he makes himself secure by putting on his own belay, and takes in any slack rope between the second and himself. The second then removes his belay, and proceeds to climb the pitch protected from above by the main ropes held by the leader. The leader takes in the ropes as the second climbs and the second removes any runners that the leader has placed.

If the original leader is to lead the next pitch, the second attaches himself to the belay before the leader takes his own belay off. The ropes can then be transferred to the second again, and the whole process repeated. If the pair are climbing alternate leads, there is, of course, no need to exchange belays. The second man climbs through to become the leader, collecting and sorting any protection slings he might need from his partner as he passes the belay.

If three climbers are on the same rope, things are more complicated. It is sometimes necessary for the leader to vacate the first belay before the third man arrives there; this will happen if the stance is too small to hold three people, or if the belay is suspect. Anyway, there will be much swapping of belays, and a rope of three can be expected to move at less than half the speed of a rope of two.

On those rare occasions when climbers are involved in climbing downwards (reversing), the order of the climbers is reversed, with the strongest climber being last. Where this happens, it is important that the first person down puts on runners to protect the last person's descent, for he is leading in reverse. There is very little of this type of climbing to be found, however, as nearly all descent on difficult rock is by abseil.

The climber here is leading the crux of Phantom Rib on Clogwyn y Grochan in the Llanberis Pass. A classic Very Severe route which requires steadiness on the part of the leader.

Communication

It is important that leader and second have a good understanding with each other about rope handling, and particularly about belaying. Most of the time there is little problem, since the second can see every move that the leader makes. Where a climb involves long pitches, with the climbers out of sight of one another, things can be more difficult. It is common practice for climbers to inform their partners of their actions by a series of calls, of which six are used commonly. When the leader has completed a pitch and is secured to the rock he will call down to his second 'Belayed!'. After a pause of a few seconds, he gives another call, 'Taking In!', and proceeds to take in any of the rope between himself and the second which has not been run out on the pitch. Obviously, if the pitch has been a long one, there will only be a small amount to take in, but if the rope they are using is 150 feet long and the pitch has only been 20 feet, then he must take in 130 feet of slack!

When the rope tightens the second responds with 'That's me'; the leader replies 'Climb when you're ready'. The second then removes his belay and calls 'Climbing'. He should feel the ropes taken in with every upward move. It is not the idea that he should be pulled up by the rope; he should have just a couple of inches of slack rope so that he knows he's climbing! If for some reason he gets into difficulties, he can warn the leader of this with a cry of 'Tight Rope'. In a similar vein, it is sometimes necessary to call 'Slack!', perhaps before making a sudden move upwards (by the leader), or a move down to a resting position. The important thing is that each climber should know what the other is doing. It will help if, when climbing in normal easy conditions, the climbers give pre-arranged signals by tugging the ropes to augment the traditional calls. In this way, they establish rapport with each other, and are much more likely to be understood on those occasions where the leader is completely out of contact with his second by voice, because of long run outs and high wind.

With most rock climbing, it is possible to avoid shouting at all, and all the better for that! A simple thumbs up signal between leader and second suffices, and makes our climbing less intrusive on others.

Artificial Climbing

On some of the big mountain routes of the world, long natural lines occur which are impossible to climb using free climbing techniques. This may be because the line is interrupted by huge overhangs. To make a climb possible, artificial

Above *A modern, hard gritstone climb, L'Horla on Curbar Edge near Sheffield. The climber, Ron Fawcett, has put on plenty of protection (photo: Rob Matheson).*

Above right:
Aid Climbing. This climber is being held in tension by his ropes before attempting a difficult move up the arête. He is standing with his left foot in a sling and has this tucked behind him to improve his balance. This pitch is on the Campanile Brabante climb in the Dolomites (grade VI) which was first climbed by Leopold, King of the Belgians.

Artificial climbing. Pegs are driven into whatever suitable cracks are available, and the climber attaches to them tape stirrups, or étriers, with a karabiner. The main ropes are usually clipped through a second karabiner on each peg as a safeguard, and the climber is held into the peg at about waist level, either by tension from the rope or by use of a short sling known as a 'cow's tail'. This leaves his arms free to place the next peg, and he stands as high as possible in the étrier to do so.

Well, that wasn't too bad. The second shows good technique: by bridging with his feet as far from the rock face as possible he is able to stand in balance while taking off a runner, thus saving on precious arm strength.

climbing is used to overcome these obstacles. Artificial climbing involves the hammering of pegs into cracks in the rock and, by attaching tape stirrups or *étrier* to these, the climber is able to conquer the biggest of overhangs. Where no cracks occur naturally, expansion bolts are fitted into holes which the climber drills. In Italy particularly, artificial climbing for its own sake was very popular. Prior to the Second World War the cult of the *diretissima* was in full swing: an imaginary plumb line was dropped from the peak of a mountain, and the climbers bashed their way up it by fair means or foul! Artificial climbing for its own sake is now out of fashion, though some modern hard climbs in Yosemite use artifical techniques of necessity. Because of excessive peg damage, climbers in the United States are increasingly exhorted to use nuts wherever possible, for the sake of so-called clean climbing.

There is a sharp distinction in climbers' minds between artificial climbing and 'aid' climbing. In the latter case direct aid from pegs or nuts might only be used on one, or at most two, occasions on a pitch. It is unusual for this aid to include the use of étriers, and more often than not it is limited to a quick pull on a sling. Subsequent climbers will try to eliminate the aid to 'clean' the climb; when this has been done word is put out that the route has gone 'free'.

Artificial climbs carry their own grading system A1 to A5. Where a route classification includes these grades, it is assumed that the paraphernalia of artificial climbing should be carried.

Climbing Ethics

Today most climbers are involved in repeating ascents of established climbs, and it is clearly laid down in the guide book what aids, if any, are allowed for the ascent. The great majority of climbs have no points of aid, but it is sometimes necessary to use a peg, nutsling, or even an

August Bank Holiday Monday on that popular Welsh crag Clogwyn y Grochan—traffic jams are not only confined to the roads! These four pairs of climbers are all on diferent routes and have converged to where ledges offer stances and also belays. The leader of the rope on the right leans out on his belay to watch his second start the pitch. The second will climb twenty feet up the groove above him, and will then traverse left along the obvious line to join the leader.

expansion bolt on the first ascent in order to overcome a difficult piece of rock. Any aids of this nature will appear in the route description, and subsequent parties are allowed to use the same amount and no more. Those who use less aid than the amount allowed can congratulate themselves on doing the route in fine style.

Others, who pull up on protection slings, or use them to rest, do little harm to the climb, and have only their conscience to grapple with. But woe betide anyone found guilty of putting in illegal pegs, because they are spoiling the climb for others. An exception to this is the use of pegs to safeguard an otherwise dangerous belay.

A more contentious issue on the use of aid is chalk. In the searing summer heat to be found on the granite walls of the Yosemite Valley in California, it has been the practice for many years for climbers to carry a bag of gymnast's chalk. When a climb is used over and over again in hot conditions, the handholds become slippery with sweat, a difficulty which is alleviated if the climber's hands are repeatedly dipped in chalk. Unfortunately, this results in the holds becoming covered in the stuff, which by any standard causes defacement of the climb, and represents a fouling of the climbing environment.

The practice has spread to this country, with many indifferent climbers using chalk to boost their own standards. Some gritstone outcrops in particular have been badly defaced. Route finding, one of the challenges when doing a climb, has been eliminated, since it is now possible to follow a line of chalked holds. Sometimes, the key to a rock climb is the use of obscure handholds which normally are difficult to locate; with the use of chalk these now stand out as clearly as if they had been painted. Perhaps one of the worst aspects of chalk is its self-perpetuating quality; some climbers now claim they have to use it to overcome the slime left by previous deposits of—chalk!

However, unlike the over use of pegs, no permanent damage to the rock is made by chalk, which, if left long enough, washes off. Even so, perhaps future public opinion will be brought to bear against its use to give us clean climbing once again.

Equipment

Assuming that you are a beginner with no equipment, and wish to make a start without borrowing from others, there are three items of gear which you must have: suitable boots, first-class rope, and a good selection of protection slings. So these items will be examined first. Equipment which might be considered optional rather than essential, such as big boots, waterproofs, rucksacks, etc., will be discussed each in turn. It is of course up to you to decide priorities of purchase of these 'lesser' items, but a climbing helmet, for example, merits early consideration here.

Boots

The pioneers of the sport climbed in full leather boots and relied upon a variety of nails in a combination of patterns to keep their feet in contact with the rock. Soft iron nails such as hobs, clinkers and muggers were commonplace in the early years of this century, later these were augmented by hardened steel nails of Swiss origin—the famous Tricounis.

Nailed boots are now a thing of the past, and a good thing too. They were dangerously slippery on the harder types of rock, and caused severe erosion of footholds, as anyone who has climbed on the Milestone Buttress of Tryfan will testify. What is more, they damaged pub floors! Around the turn of the century, plimsoles were used for the first time, and an increase in the degree of difficulty, or grade, of new climbs resulted. So much so that it was usual for a climb to be given two grades; the normal one for boots, and an easier one for 'rubbers'.

After the Second World War, the cleated rubber Commando sole became available. Used on a full leather boot with substantial middle soles, this resulted in a good combination boot, suitable both for rock climbing and general mountaineering use. Boots of this type are still very widely used, and are available in a great variety of qualities and prices. They should, however, be regarded in the context of a mountaineering boot, and needn't be considered as essential equipment for today's rock climber since better, cheaper alternatives are on the market.

In the 1950s, British climbers began to use *kletterschuhe* which were imported from Austria. These 'kletts' have a suède upper and a lightweight, cleated rubber sole. They are very comfortable boots and are not expensive by today's standards, but they do not have the

'You'd have thought somebody would have invented something for a situation like this.'

Edwardian lady's climbing boot. The high, tightly-laced ankle offered good support, but to accommodate the massive nails the soles had to be strongly made and were therefore heavy. Difficult enough to climb in, they were purgatory to walk in—the shock of every stone was transmitted to the feet.

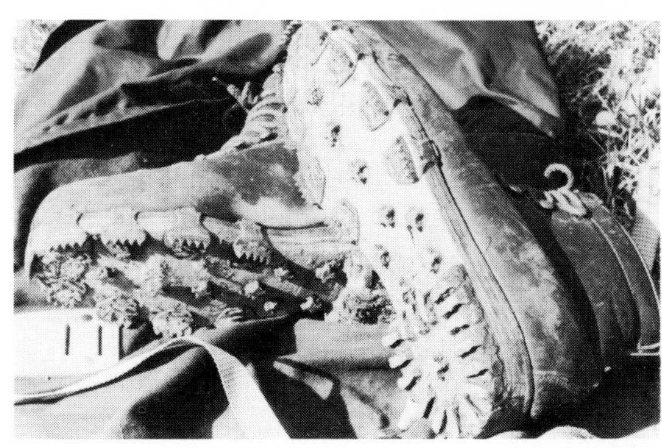

This style of mountain boot was popular until the advent of cleated rubber soles in the early '50s. The famous Tricouni No. 6 climbing nail can be seen round the welts, with muggers in the middle of the sole, and clinkers around the heel. The Tricouni could be used on the tiniest of footholds, which it promptly wore away!

Kletterschuhe. This one (by Hawkins) has a green suede upper with a lightweight Vibram Roccia sole. A comfortable general purpose rock boot, also used for occasional mountain walking. It has one big drawback—the wearer will be lucky to arrive home with dry feet as it's not waterproof.

Scarpa Trento walking boot. A semi-stiffened boot with one-piece leather upper and Vibram Montagna sole, good for walking long distances in high country in order to climb on mountain crags. Used for rock climbing because of the neat welt at the toe, but too flexible for the harder routes.

A true mountain boot, Galibier Terray Fitzroy. Well-used, this boot is showing signs of losing some of the stiffness associated with boots designed for rock climbing. The upper is of top quality, with D-rings and hooks through-rivetted.

Dolomite Super Egger. A quality mountain boot which, typical of its type, has a full-length metal shank in the sole which makes it very stiff. Designed for technical rock and ice climbing, they are not general purpose walking boots.

Super Klett, Sportiva Civetta, an updated version of the kletterschuhe, with a stiffening shank, rubber friction rand and suede upper. A good rock climbing boot, more suited to long periods of wear than the tight pure rock boot. Waterproof to top of the rand only.

EB Super Gratton, the original French 'magic boot', designed purely for rock climbing and suitable for nothing else. A favourite with British rock climbers, offering good performance and value for money.

Hawkins GTH rock boot. Another popular boot over the years, the GTH has a harder-wearing, suede upper than other types (of canvas). With a rather narrow fit, and sole rubber harder than the French rock boots, it is not in such demand.

Galibier PA. Not the original PA! (which is now the EB), it nevertheless has many of the features of its famous compatriot. It is significantly more expensive than the EB, however.

Caber Messner Rock Boot, another Super Klett. This one has more of the characteristics of the mountain boot, since it has a Montagna sole and double rivetted hooks. Like others of its type, it has a suede upper, and is really more suitable for drier climes.

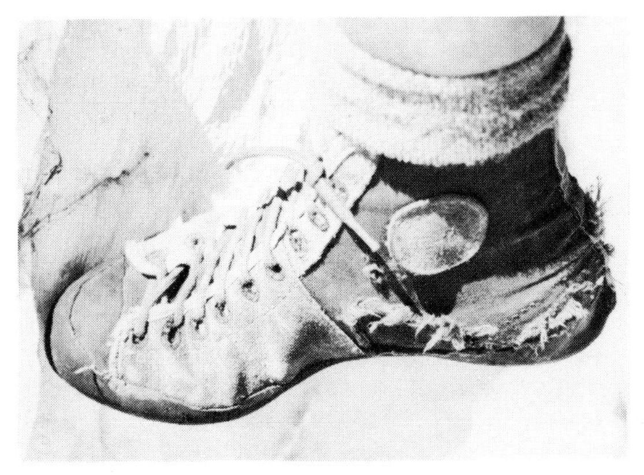

This EB has seen too much sea cliff climbing, witness the eyelets rusted by salt air; and too much scree, hence the tatty canvas upper. But the owner is convinced that there's good climbing to be had from his boots yet.

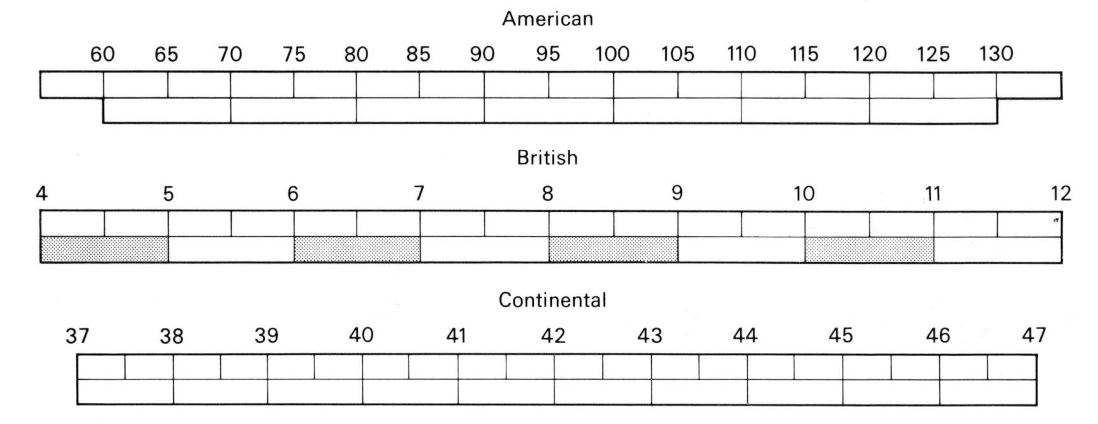

Chart giving comparison of boot sizing.

performance of the modern rock boot and so have slowly fallen from favour.

Virtually all British rock climbers now use one of several makes of specialist rock boots, and indeed might climb for years without owning a 'big' boot of any sort. The rock boot had its origin in France and represented a breakthrough in design. This was the original PA, which under its changed initials of EB remains easily the most popular rock boot in the world. There have been a number of attempts to emulate the performance of this type, including a design from Galibier (named PA to add to the confusion), but the original seems to have exactly the right combination of desirable qualities: ideal foot shape, good flexibility, cling rubber, and a relatively low price. Ninety per cent of rock boots used in Britain are EBs and all those climbers can't be wrong! They have a completely smooth sole with a shallow, pointed toe. Their most important feature is the rubber friction band surrounding the welt, which ensures that the boot maintains its close-fitting shape throughout its life, as well as providing valuable friction when toe jamming.

The material of the uppers varies from boot to boot. In the EB it is of stout canvas, in other types it might be suède leather or some combination of the two. In order to ensure a close fit, a rock boot laces from low on the toe right up to the ankle.

Climbers still sometimes take the business of close fit for their rock boots too far. It once used to be believed that unless physical pain resulted from wearing boots, they couldn't be a close enough fit, and as a consequence climbing performance would suffer. Indeed, at one time PA feet was threatening to become as endemic to climbing as tennis elbow is to that sport! Good sense now prevails and most climbers agree that foot comfort is important when rock climbing. It is also now common practice to wear thick socks, whereas ten years ago no socks were worn. It is as well to know something of European sizing when purchasing boots and comparisons can be made with the help of the above table.

It should be pointed out that the pure rock boot is totally unsuited to mountain walking; quite apart from the uncomfortably tight fit, the smooth sole is dangerously slippery on wet grass or mud, and the canvas upper quickly suffers when crossing scree. Some walking is inevitable, for example when descending after completion of a climb, and great care is required here since a number of fatalities have occurred to climbers who have slipped while wearing smooth-soled boots. No doubt a contributory factor in these circumstances has been a relaxation of concentration after the tension of a climb.

Half a lifetime can be spent by the rock climber on crags within easy reach of the road if he so wishes, and therefore it is not necessary to purchase an expensive mountain boot to begin with. However, if you want to visit the more remote mountain crags in Britain, some form of boot with a substantial cleated sole will be necessary to guarantee foothold on steep and wet mountainsides. A cheap, fell boot will suffice, or you can choose one of the many standard walking boots available on the British market, such as the Scarpa Trento. These are less than half the price of a top-class mountain boot such as the Super RD and are much better suited to hill walking.

A recent development which might be considered is the Superklett. This is a medium weight boot which has the cleated sole of the mountain boot, the rubber rand of the rock boot, and the upper of a klett. Thus it is possible to walk to a mountain crag in safety, and climb to a reasonable standard in the same boot. Critics of these boots say that, like all compromises, they cannot achieve excellence in any one respect and are a poor rock boot married to a worse walking boot! Perhaps they are better suited to their intended purpose—long, dry rock climbs where brief encounters with snow or ice cannot be ruled out. There are many such routes on the Continent which are too long to endure the discomfort of a pure rock boot, but which are technically too difficult for the stiff and heavy mountain boot.

So buy a rock boot, and the EB is probably the best as well as being the cheapest; defer the purchase of a mountain boot until a sound decision can be taken in the light of experience, and if necessary buy a sensible walking boot if you propose to venture to mountain crags, or combine rock climbing with mountain walking as a sport.

Climbing Ropes

The second item which is absolutely essential is the climbing rope. It is the most important piece of equipment which a climber possesses, and must be well cared for. It shouldn't be lent out, trodden upon, or used as a tow rope. It should be stored in a dry place, out of sunlight, and away from such things as car battery acid, for your life might depend on it. If it is damaged by falling stones or sustains a severe fall, it should be discarded in the interests of safety, since serious damage may have occurred without this fact being obvious. Climbing ropes are now such costly items that it pays to look after them. A rope's life, of course, depends on the amount of use it gets. For the average climber this will amount to about 20,000 feet of climbing per annum, and at this pace a rope should be pensioned off after two to three years.

Main ropes. There are two sizes of rope used in climbing, and it is important to understand the fundamental difference in their use before considering purchase. Generally speaking, European climbers favour the use of two 9-mm diameter ropes, whilst Americans prefer a single 11-mm rope. There are some climbers who use double ropes in a combination of 9/11 mm, and a small number who use double 11 mm, though rope weight and drag become rather excessive in the latter case.

Apart from the increase in initial cost, the advantages of using double ropes are many, and are briefly summarized here:

1. Descent by abseil can be twice the distance of that which can be made with a single rope.
2. When climbing, the two ropes can be led through different lines of runners in order to minimize drag.
3. Better protection can be given to the second when traversing; one of the ropes can also be used as a back rope for the same purpose.

A clutch of ropes. When buying, look carefully at the labels. Of these five (which are all 11-mm diameter), one does not meet the UIAA specification and so cannot carry the UIAA label; the others are rated as 3-fall, 4-fall, 7-fall and 9-fall ropes. Yet the 9-fall rope is the second cheapest.

4. There is less risk of two ropes being cut by stonefall.
5. In the event of a leader fall there is less risk of both ropes being cut by sawing over a rock edge.
6. Greater versatility is possible when climbing as a rope of three.
7. There are also advantages of rope usage and replacement, i.e. each of a pair of climbers can both supply and carry one rope.

Italian hemp was the best rope available to the early climbers, and natural fibres such as manilla were also used until the discovery of long chain polymers in the 1940s. Subsequently, hawser laid nylon rope became generally available as climbing rope from 1950 onwards; it is still widely used today where cost is a consideration. Its very great advantages over natural fibres are: twice the tensile strength for a given weight, much improved modulus of elasticity, and pleasanter handling qualities when wet.

White hawser laid rope is manufactured in four standard sizes, numbered 1 to 4. The two smaller sizes are hardly used now, but the No. 3 (10 mm) and the No. 4 (11 mm) are still in demand by outdoor education centres for instructional purposes, for which they are ideal. Beyond the information on static breaking load, no information concerning performance is available, however, and their use by rock climbers has declined greatly. The cost of hawser laid rope is at present about two-thirds that of kernmantel rope of similar diameter, but it is not advisable to use it with the latest mechanical rope ascending and belay devices, which tend to make the strands separate.

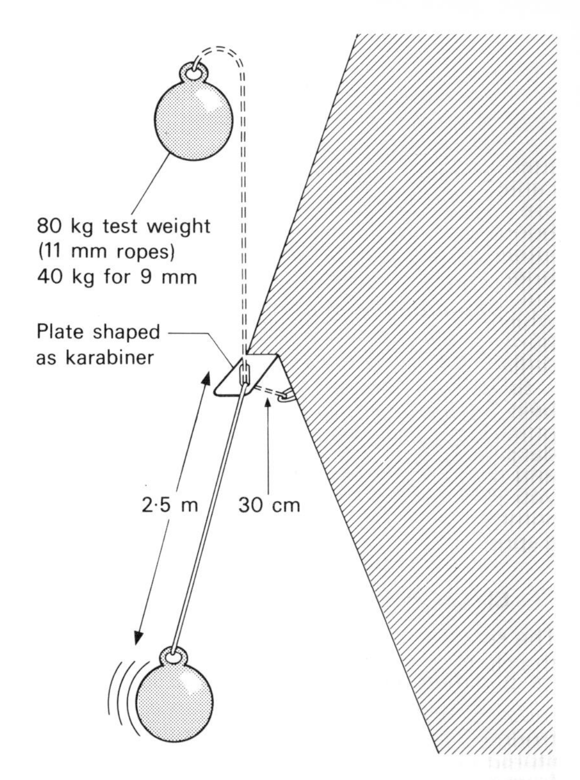

Dodero Drop Test *This is the standard UIAA test for climbing ropes. A severe fall is simulated by dropping a weight of 80 kg a distance of 5 m. In order to carry the UIAA label, a rope must be capable of holding 3 such falls without breaking. The best of today's ropes sustain 13 falls (11 mm single) and 20 falls (9 mm double).*

Double 9-mm kernmantel. It is now compulsory for ropes carrying the UIAA label to have the ends marked with a ½ or 1, depending on whether intended for use as double or single ropes. Rope diameters are approximate only, and a recent fatality occurred when a 9-mm rope was used as single rope by mistake.

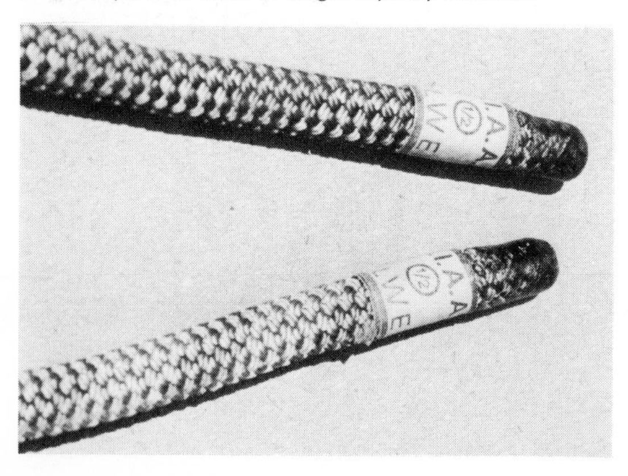

The vast majority of climbing ropes in use are of the kernmantel type, consisting of many thousands of parallel fibres enclosed in a braided sheath. The performance of a rope can be designed into it, depending on such factors as material used and core construction: some ropes have their cores stranded so that the sheath encloses several smaller ropes, whilst in others the fibres are laid side by side throughout the length of the rope. In a climbing rope, elasticity is an advantage since it minimizes the impact force on the belay chain, and yet too much stretch cannot be tolerated because it increases the distance fallen by the climber. Another design criterion, though not so important, is that there should be low initial stretch under light loads. The object of this is to minimize wasted effort in rope climbing where much prusiking is involved, i.e. on very big climbs where only one person climbs the rock and the others climb the rope.

These conflicting demands have now been met through developments over the last fifteen years: today's best ropes typically consist of a core of 50,000 threads contained in a sheath of 25,000 threads! With various claims and counter-claims being made by manufacturers for their ropes, it became necessary to devise a standard drop test in order to effect comparison, and to this end the UIAA has adopted the Dodero Test. This is of real value, since to carry the UIAA label the maker must clearly state the fall holding capability of the rope. This must be a minimum of three falls to carry the label at all, but in the case of some modern 11-mm ropes might be as many as twelve falls. Thus there is a considerable spectrum of performance found amongst ropes selling at similar prices, indeed it is possible to pay 20 per cent more for a rope which will sustain half the number of falls of its competitor. The situation with 9-mm ropes is comparable but not so clear. In the UIAA test the tacit assumption is made that in the event of a fall on double ropes, each rope wil be subjected to half the load. Since in certain circumstances one rope only of the two will be stressed, this idea is erroneous. However, these ropes are tested with only half the drop weight, and consequently score very highly. Many will be seen to hold twenty falls by this testing method, and it is not easy to sort the good from the bad. It is a good idea to compare the various makers' results with 11-mm ropes when buying 9-mm since they use the same yarns and techniques with each type. This is where the retailers' advice can be sought, as they take a keen interest and will often give advice without prejudice on all climbing equipment.

Some ropes are marketed with 'Superdry' or 'Everdry' as part of the description on the label. These have been chemically treated to repel water. The reason for this is that kernmantel ropes are likely to absorb upwards of 20 per cent of their weight of water when used in wet conditions. Apart from the disadvantage of sheer weight, a loss of rope strength occurs which in freezing conditions can be as much as 40 per cent, which is clearly serious. Some of the ropes are offered with this treatment at no extra cost, which is a factor to be borne in mind, particularly if winter climbing or Alpine routes are contemplated.

Another problem which faces the prospective rope buyer is which length of rope to purchase. With the 11-mm single rope there is little difficulty, since most ropes sold are 45 metres (or 150 feet). Sometimes there is a demand for 50-metre ropes, particularly for climbing in Yosemite valley, USA, where this length is much used.

The purchaser of a 9-mm double rope is faced with the choice of either two lengths of 45 metres (or, rarely, 50 metres as above) or a single length of 90 metres. The 90-metre length's one advantage is when it is used for abseil. Where two 45-metre lengths are used for a long abseil, they have to be knotted at the anchor point and when all the party have descended, the rope is pulled down from below.

Most climbers are prepared to accept the risk of the knot snagging for the greater convenience of handling two separate ropes which are much easier to keep free of kinks. A further point is the matter of rope colour: clearly it is important to distinguish between double ropes by using different colours, but the 90-metre length with a colour change halfway is expensive to make and buy.

A good way of keeping a rope is to chain plait it and carry it in this fashion. Coiling a rope means twisting it many times, putting kinks into it; if a rope is plaited in this manner it can then be used without the tiresome business of sorting it out.

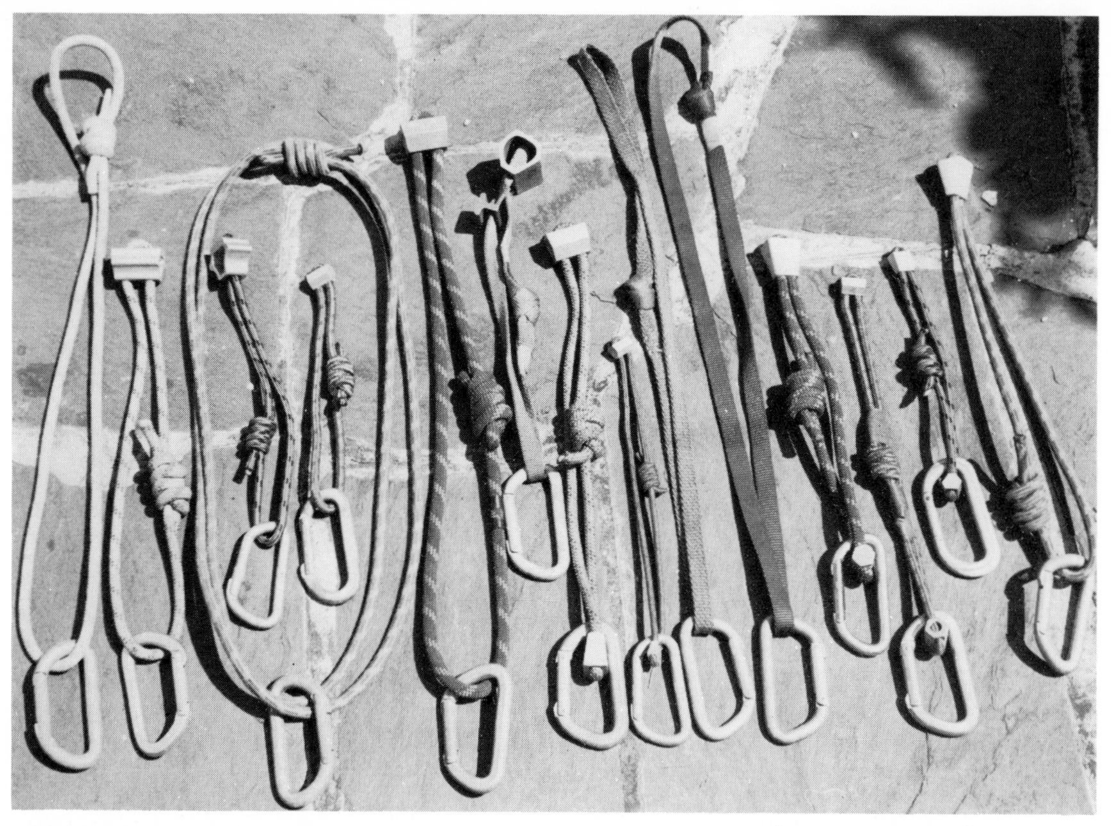

One man's protection: a variety of plain slings and nut slings; several small wedges on wire will usually be carried as well. Some of this climber's slings carry a nut at each end in order to offer a greater variety of placement, a practice which weakens the sling somewhat. It is sensible to match the sling with a karabiner of similar strength. A double fisherman's knot is used on the rope slings, a tape knot on the tape slings. Tapes have their loose ends bound with electrical tape (or can be stitched) to prevent slippage.

The beginner then, assuming he couldn't climb with, or share, someone else's ropes, would be well advised to buy a pair of 45-metre 9-mm ropes of good specification and of different colours.

Protection Slings

A favourite, personal part of every rock climber's gear is his 'protection', i.e. slings. Apart from the implicit protection from main rope, a climber will carry up to twenty slings for use as running belays, which the leader places as he climbs. In their simplest form, these are slings of rope or tape attached to natural rock spikes, and the main rope is held by the sling via a metal karabiner. In the event of a fall, the climber will be held from his highest protection sling rather than from his belay which might be far below.

About six of the twenty slings will be of the 'plain' type, intended for use in belay work, thread runners, or rock spike runners. They might include a couple of sound offcuts of discarded 9-mm rope, and will include slings of 5-mm and 7-mm diameter for use in narrow cracks or on small spikes. These 'line' slings are also used for prusiking. Specially designed nylon tapes have been available for some years as runner slings; these have the advantage of resistance to rolling off rounded rock spikes and can be bought with the joint stitched rather than knotted. Stitched slings are stronger than knotted, and are generally more convenient to use. At least one long sling (8 feet circumference) should be carried for belay work, the others ideally being about half as long.

The remainder of the slings carried should be 'nut' slings, used for jamming. In the old days, it wasn't unknown for a climber to knot a sling, and jam the knot into a suitable crack to provide a welcome runner. Indeed a famous party attempting what they thought to be the first British ascent of that formidable alpine classic, the Walker Spur, knew that they had been beaten to it when, nearing the summit, they found an abandoned jammed knot sling, a sure sign that other Britons had beaten them to it, and so it chanced to be!

Just who first threaded an ordinary machine nut onto a sling, with the idea of jamming it into a crack for protection, remains a mystery, but there is no doubt that this idea revolutionized protection methods the world over. Apocryphal stories were told of machines in Midlands car factories breaking down for want of nuts stolen by rapacious climbers! It was usual to have four or five sizes of nut on the same sling in order to offer a choice of placement, and the slings were always carried around the neck in the way that 'plain' slings are now.

The jammed nut idea proved to be so effective that there were specially manufactured nuts on the market within a short time. The early ones imitated their machine nut forebears by having a hexagonal section, though they were made from aluminium. Later ones were wedge-shaped, and others 'hexentric', being designed to cam in parallel-sided cracks. The demand for protection in ever tinier cracks resulted in smaller sizes of nuts being provided with a swaged wire sling attached.

However bewildering the variety, nuts are basically hexagonal or wedge-shaped. Every climber has his favourites which he doesn't like to be without. The older types (as at bottom right) imitated their machine nut forebears; later came a lop-sided 'hexentric' type which were designed to 'cam' in parallel cracks (centre). With the demand for protection for increasingly difficult moves, smaller and smaller wedges were developed; below a certain size, it is necessary to use a wire sling on these.

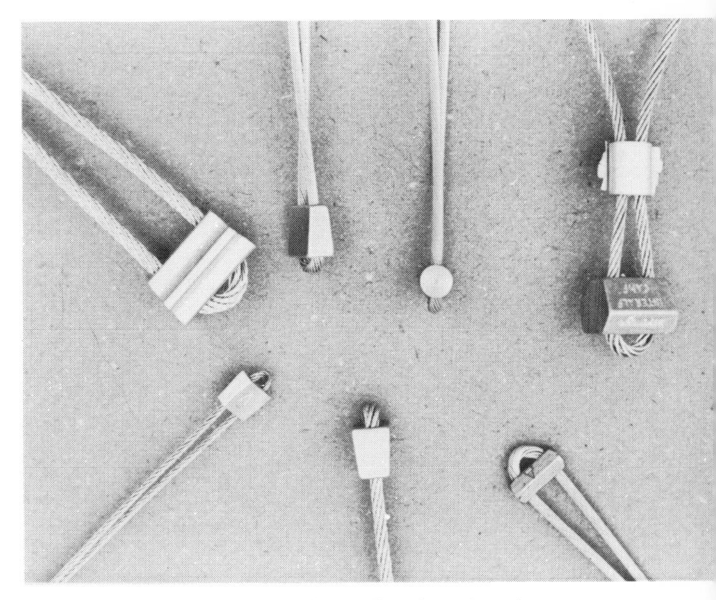

Wired slings. Popular mostly in smaller sizes, the wires vary considerably in flexibility. Because a stiff wire tends to cause the nut to lift out as the leader climbs above it, it is a good idea to examine carefully what is available.

When a wire sling is used, it is usual to attach to it a short tape-loop about a foot long in order to prevent the stiff wire sling from lifting out of the crack as the climber moves up. Ideally, a karabiner should be used between wire and tape since the small radius of the wire reduces the breaking strain of the tape dramatically.

It is usual to keep nutslings short whether they are wire or rope; most climbers seem to prefer a sling a foot or so in length and will carry a variety to suit their particular requirements. Ten to fifteen slings are the number normally carried, many people preferring to 'rack' them on a bandolier or, more commonly, on the gear loops attached for the purpose on the sit harness. Orderly climbers rack their nutslings in the same places every time they climb, and can thus locate a particular wedge or hexentric without looking or fumbling, very important when you are trying to place protection from a strenuous position.

Other Protection Devices

A recent development in protection equipment is a mechanical device known as Friends. They have opposing cams which, when inserted into a crack, spring out and grip the rock. A sling is attached to the stem of the device, and in the event of a fall the shock loading opens out the cams to grip the rock harder. They are said to be capable of

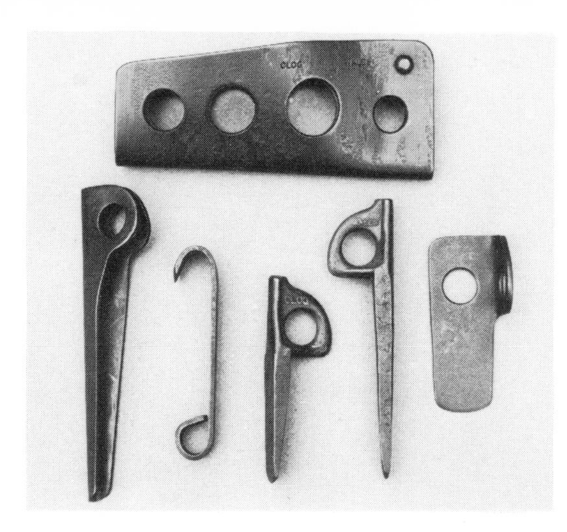

Modern pegs. Made from hardened steel alloys, they far outlast the older, mild steel ones, but they also cause more damage to the rock. At the top is a 'bong bong' which has replaced the wooden wedge. An angle peg is at the bottom of the picture, followed by a skyhook, two king pins and an offset blade.

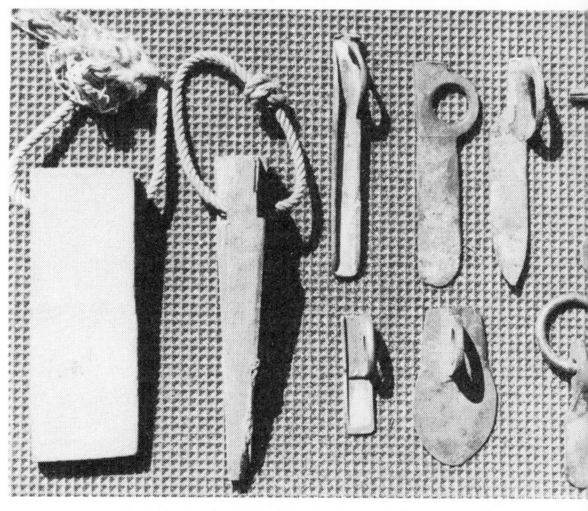

Some interesting older pegs. From left to right, wooden wedges, now hardly used; across the top, channel, blade and offset pegs. At top right is an expansion bolt; below this the modern 'Realised Ultimate Reality Piton', (RURP for short—Are You Har-ppy). At the bottom: a small channel, an ace of spades, and finally a ring peg designed for abseiling.

Peg Hammers. Since many rock climbers also climb on ice in winter, many choose a peg hammer with a curved pick which doubles as an ice hammer.

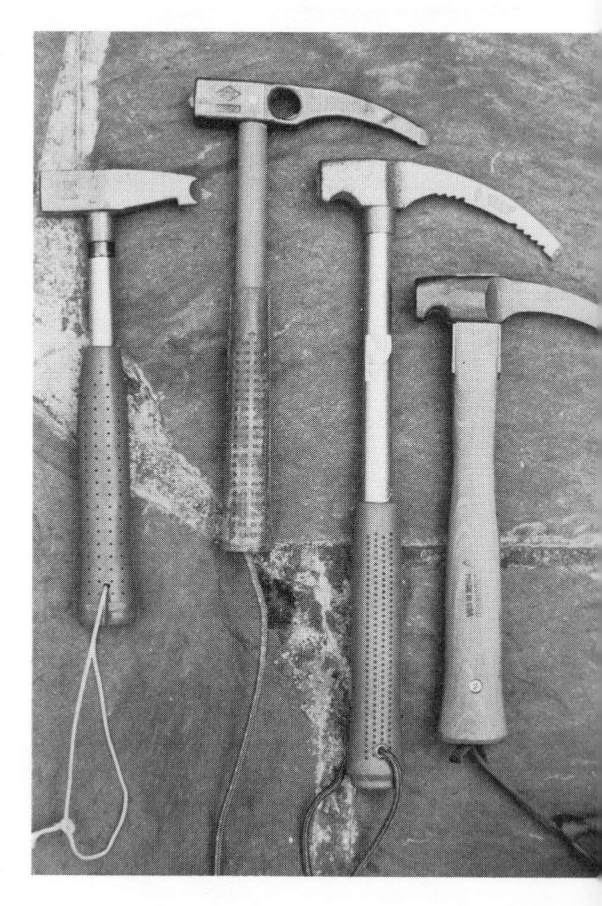

holding moderate falls. However, they have been subjected to criticism by some climbers who feel that mechanical devices are not fair play because they take the risk factor out of climbing, to the detriment of the sport.

A much older (and even more contentious) item in the climbing protection 'racket' is the metal peg or piton. As most people know, these are intended to be driven into suitable cracks in the rock and will provide reliable protection when nothing else is available. The problem is that repeated use of pegs, and particularly the hard alloy steel variety, damages the rock extensively. It is obviously easy for people to destroy the pleasure of others by use of pegs where they are not necessary. Until very recently this has been a real problem in the United States, where use of pegs was tacitly accepted. The development of nuts for protection, coupled with a drive for 'clean climbing' has somewhat alleviated the problem there, though little can be done about those routes already heavily peg-scarred.

In Britain the use of pegs has virtually been brought to a halt. But, their use as belays to safeguard otherwise dangerous stances has long been accepted, and where pegs are used in this way they will often be left *in situ* for the benefit of

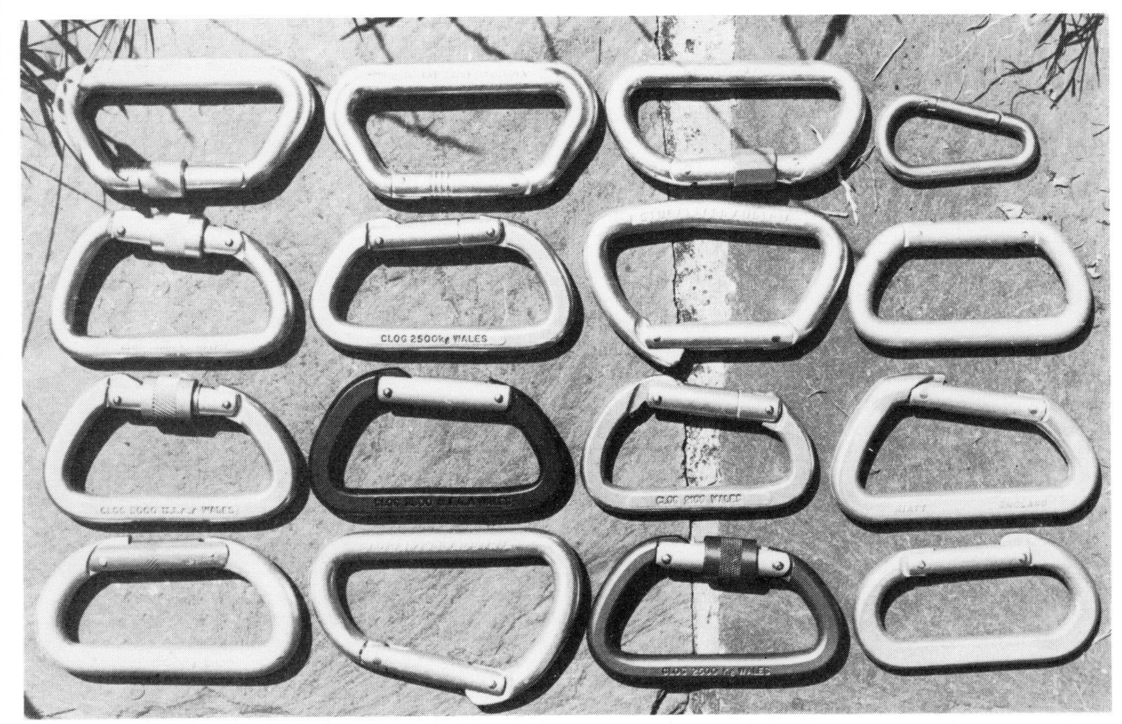

Some karabiners. Nearly all are aluminium alloy, and some have screw keepers to prevent accidental opening of the gate. They are mostly D-shaped so that under stress, ropes will slip into the corners away from the weak gate; they are tested under fairly ideal circumstances with a steel bar in each corner, but in an actual climbing incident the presence of several ropes in the karabiner could cause more severe loading of the gate than that simulated in the test.

Some old karabiner designs; all are made of steel. The second from the right is the notorious Ex War Dept karabiner, some examples of which are reputed to have broken at 500 lbs load.

other climbers. In those rare cases where a peg might be used for protection, or direct aid, on a new climb, it is again customary to leave it in place, and where this is so it is entered in the route description. But because of the force of climbing opinion, most rock climbers no longer carry hammers and pegs, and it would be pointless for the beginner to buy them.

Karabiners

Karabiners, to use their German and adopted British name, have been used in rock climbing for

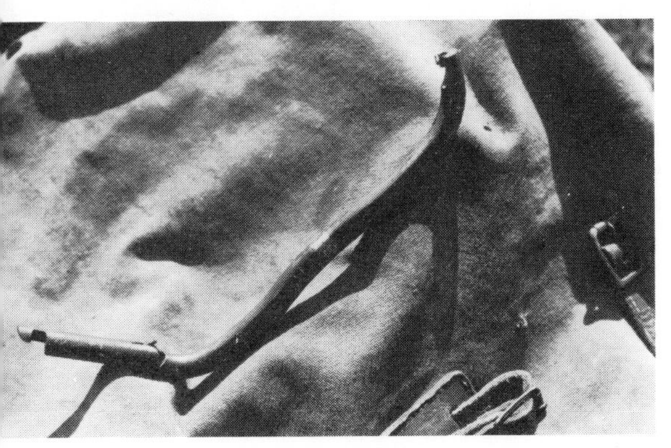

One that got away. This was a steel D-shaped krab, found at the foot of a crag. Subjected to a fall, the gate has opened and the ropes have slipped out; the vicious hook of the gate at the right side will probably have caused serious damage to the rope. Modern karabiners are stronger.

over fifty years and have a multiplicity of uses. In appearance the karabiner ('krab') is a large chain link with a spring gate on one of the longer sides. Modern karabiners are made from aircraft type aluminium alloys in order to minimize weight, and the great majority are now D-shaped. The object of this shape is to concentrate shock loads on the relatively strong spine of the krab, and away from the weaker gate.

There are many types of karabiner on the market. Most of the manufacturers stamp on to the spines the breaking strains in kilogrammes. A UIAA standard is in existence which stipulates that a karabiner should sustain a load of 2200 kg along the major axis, and 600 kg across the shorter axis. In practice, many of the more popular karabiners available do not achieve the standard because of a technicality concerned with a different part of the test, but such lightweight karabiners as the Clog 2100, or the Bonaiti 2000 offer a good combination of strength for price, and are more likely to match the strength of the runners than the stronger, heavier, and more expensive UIAA approved ones.

A beginner would be advised to purchase about ten of the lightweight variety, with a further three or four made up of a combination of 2500 and 3000 kg karabiners, of which a couple of the latter should have a screw keeper to prevent accidental gate opening when used for belays or abseils.

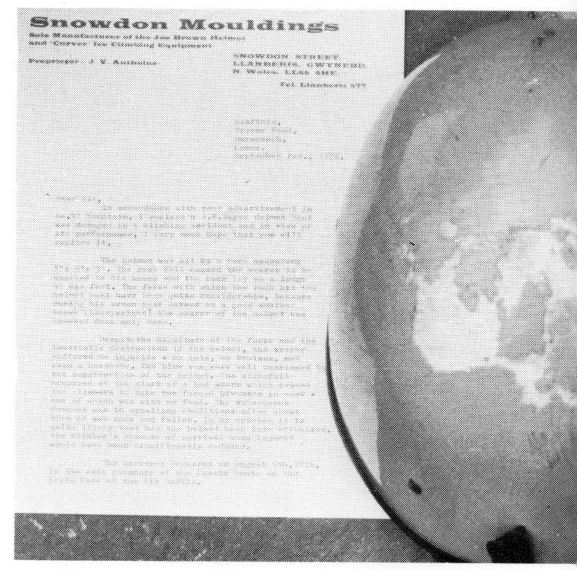
Snowdon Mouldings
Sole Manufacturer of the Joe Brown Helmet
and 'Curver' Ice Climbing Equipment
Proprietor: J. V. Anthoine
SNOWDON STREET,
LLANBERIS, GWYNEDD,
N. Wales, LL55 4HE
Tel. Llanberis 377

If you want to keep your head. . . . The life of the wearer of this helmet was saved when he was hit on the head by a stone the size of a house brick.

Helmets

A climbing helmet fulfils two clearly defined functions: it protects the wearer's head from falling stones, and it protects his head from injury through contact with the rock in the event of a fall.

There is by no means universal acceptance of the helmet as an essential piece of climbing equipment. Some climbers feel that the general discomfort and inconvenience of wearing one downgrade the climbing experience, and that the small risk of injury is more than outweighed by the pleasant feel of sun and wind on the head. Another school states that helmets should be worn at all times whether there is any apparent danger or not. Perhaps the real answer lies somewhere between the two extremes: wear a helmet if you judge that there is obvious danger of stonefall (this might particularly apply to high, loose crags where other parties are climbing above you).

The only construction which appears to be satisfactory at present for climbing helmets is glassfibre. Recent tests carried out on behalf of the German Alpine Club show that cheaper helmets made by vacuum-forming ABS plastic do not approach the strength requirements for a proposed standard, and that this material quickly reduces in strength as freezing point is approached.

When buying a helmet it is important to ensure that a good fit is obtained, since an ill-fitting helmet will prove irksome and the inclination will be not to wear it at all. Various sizes are available and the headband is adjustable to give a snug fit.

Helmets are sized, and each has an adjustable headband. Most have a foam liner which contributes to their strength, but the one on the bottom left is unlined to save a little weight. All have a glass fibre shell. British-made helmets are among the best.

Belts and Harnesses

Although there are a few climbing diehards who still tie directly on to the main ropes, most climbers now use some sort of harness around their body to which the main ropes are then attached. The simplest form is the climber's belt, which is merely a broad band of nylon webbing covered in canvas. Attachment to the main rope is via a D-ring which slides freely on the belt. This belt does have some advantages over the direct tie; it is simpler to use when instructing children and risk of the belt melting is reduced when used as a dynamic waist belay, but it is doubtful if it is effective in preventing damage to the climber's body in a fall.

Continental climbers have always favoured the chest tie, rather than the waist tie preferred by the British, and choice of harnesses follows suit. Exponents of the chest harness maintain that a fallen climber (who might be unconscious), is more likely to remain in an upright position when suspended from a point higher up on his body, and that there is less danger of injury to the climber's back than when using a 'sit' harness. The British argue that in a large number of experimental falls, climbers wearing chest harnesses invariably finished with the head hanging backwards, chin uppermost—with a real risk of suffocation. There is the additional unpleasant prospect of being bashed in the face by the conglomeration of knots just under the chin, and any metalwear which also happens to be present at that point.

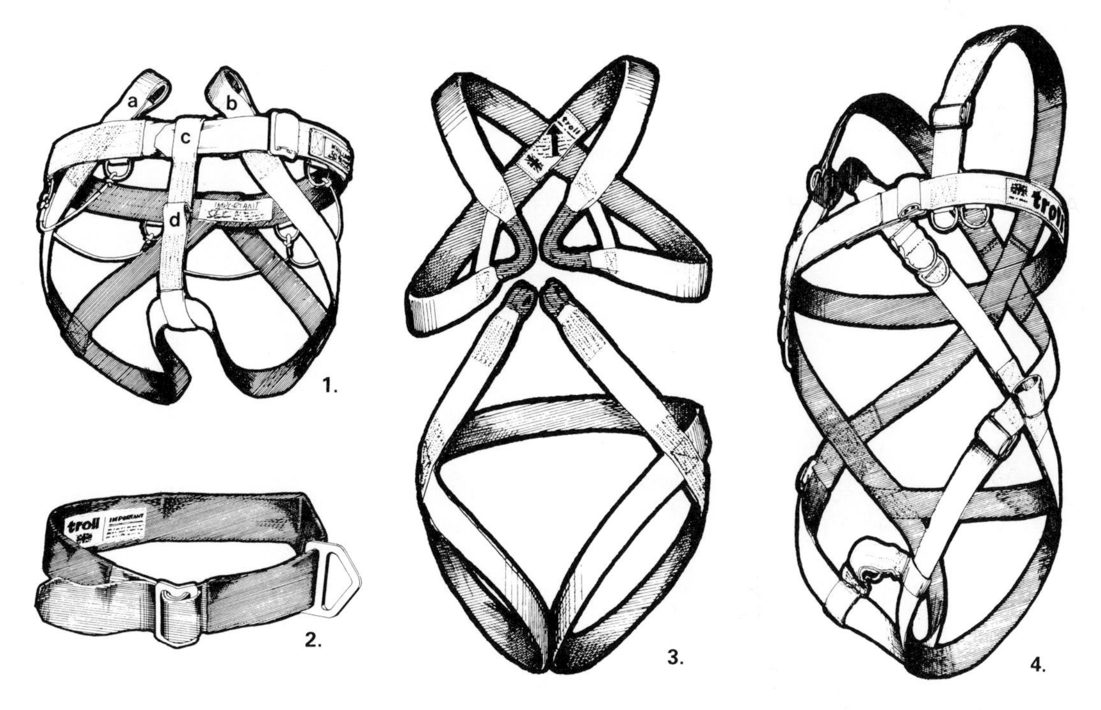

1. Whillans Sit Harness *(frontal view), easily the most popular climbing harness used in Britain. The main ropes are threaded through the three loops* a, b, c, *and fastened with a bowline or Figure 8 on the bight. A screw gate karabiner is clipped through loop* d *and the main ropes pass through this. If the climber falls he is automatically held in a sitting position.*
2. Climbers' Belt *A modern alternative to the direct waist tie, or tape swami belt. Security of the belt fastening depends on the end of the belt being returned through the buckle after being threaded in the normal way; this also applies to the Whillans harness. Attachment of the climbing ropes is by a screw gate karabiner on to the sliding D ring.*
3. Klimelite Body Harness. *A lightweight two-piece body harness. The main ropes are tied on through the four loops which meet at the chest. This harness has no method of adjustment, but is available in a comprehensive range of sizes. It is relatively inexpensive.*
4. Troll Full Body Harness *This substantial harness weighs 2 lb (900 g). It is designed with proposed UIAA standards for harnesses in mind, and is fully adjustable. Tie in at the two loops at chest level. Shock loads are transmitted via the long diagonal straps to the strong pelvic region. The D rings which can be seen are intended as equipment carriers; a hammer holster is fitted as standard. General feeling among rock climbers is that this harness is too heavy and cumbersome, though undoubtedly effective.*

These are the main reasons why the sit harness is virtually the only harness in demand by British climbers at present. There are a couple of full body harness designs on the market, which combine in some measure the virtues of both sit and chest harness, and one of these, the Klimelite, has advantages of simplicity and price, but it doesn't appeal to many climbers. Easily the most popular harness in use is the Whillans sit harness, and about seven climbers out of ten in Britain are wearing them. As tribute to its effectiveness, after a recent fall on the Welsh cliff of Cyrn Las, a climber was able to dangle for over four hours in his Whillans harness in reasonable comfort until extricated from his predicament. Compare this with the oft-quoted figure for a climber hanging from a direct tie onto his waist: fifteen minutes to unconsciousness, and another fifteen to death!

Back view of the Whillans Sit Harness (see illustration 1. previous page).

Troll 'Klimelite' two-piece harness. Light and simple, this harness is made in a variety of sizes to ensure proper fit (there is no adjustment on the harness). The main rope is tied through the four loops in front of the climber's chest; note that these are sleeved with canvas to eliminate the danger of them melting under shock loading.

There are some additional, fringe benefits to the wearing of a harness. Rock climbers are now carrying more equipment in the form of nutslings and karabiners, and most harnesses are festooned with equipment loops to hang these from. It is also easy to attach hammer holsters for peg hammer, or perhaps ice axes if you are snow and ice climbing.

Waterproofs and Windproofs

Naturally enough, not many rock climbers like to climb in the rain when, apart from the general unpleasantness associated with such weather, the climbs become much more difficult due to greasy rock conditions. Wind can pose a problem to climbers by what is termed chill factor, particularly when long periods are spent by individuals on belay ledges. The rock climber's answer to both these problems is one and the same—to carry a lightweight, pull-over-the-head garment—the cagoule.

In its simplest form it is a cheap two-ounce Bri-Nylon anorak without pockets or zips but with a hood, and it packs so small that it can be carried in a trouser pocket, or more commonly rolled up and worn around the waist tied by its sleeves. A garment like this can be a godsend on a cold, windy day because of its very good windproof

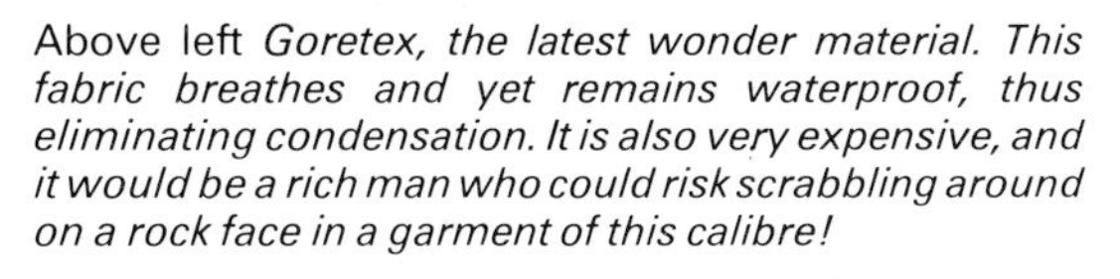

Above left *Goretex, the latest wonder material. This fabric breathes and yet remains waterproof, thus eliminating condensation. It is also very expensive, and it would be a rich man who could risk scrabbling around on a rock face in a garment of this calibre!*

Above centre *A more substantial waterproof, the Berghaus 'Thor' jacket. This is neoprene proofed 4-oz nylon and has a zip front with two large patch pockets. It is quite waterproof, though obviously more bulky and more expensive than the basic cagoule.*

Above right *A basic lightweight cagoule, made from 2-oz polyurethane-proofed nylon. This is a good choice for the rock climber, being light, cheap and windproof. It will pack so small as to be unnoticed until needed.*

Right *The best waterproof overtrousers have long zips so that they may be put on over the boots.*

qualities, and if its waterproof qualities leave something to be desired it will at least keep the wearer dry for half an hour or so while he extracts himself from his climb if caught in the rain!

Of course, there are many other types of waterproof which an individual might choose rather than the ultra-lightweight variety; for instance, if you are interested in winter hill walking as well as rock climbing, you may decide that a four-ounce or eight-ounce cagoule (these are weights per square yard of material) would better suit your needs.

Although the pullover type is more suited to a purely rock climbing role, many people prefer a zip-fronted jacket for more general hill walking duties, because it is possible to ventilate such a garment easily by having the front partly unzipped. The reason for wanting good ventilation, of course, is to cut down condensation on the inside of the garment—a bugbear with all impermeable materials.

There is a considerable variation in performance amongst the waterproof materials available to the rock climber, and it is as well to try to establish in your mind the level of usage and quality of the garment required, otherwise you might pay a very high price for a jacket which is heavy, bulky and stiff, and therefore unsuitable for the chief purpose for which it was bought. Of the lower-priced materials, polyurethane (PU) proofing is the cheapest, but has a shorter life than neoprene proofing. Both of these are applied to Bri-Nylon garments. The other thing to look for in this type of waterproof is the type of seaming used. First check that all possible seams in the vulnerable shoulder and neck areas have been eliminated by intelligent use of the material. The remaining seams will have been made up in a variety of ways: rolled seam; rolled and doped; bound with a separate piece of material; or taped internally. Each of these is a more expensive production process than the one preceding it, and whereas a simple pull-over cagoule, PU-proofed with rolled seams, can be bought for a few pounds, the neoprene-proofed, zipped jacket with taped seams is nearly £30.

There are other materials to be considered. Cotton anoraks have much to recommend them since they have a more pleasant feel than the Bri-Nylon type. It is still possible to buy a double-texture cotton twill anorak for £12 or so, and if re-proofed annually in a bucket of 'Nev' will give many years of service. Rather a different kettle of fish is cotton 'Ventile' cloth which is about the most expensive waterproof on the market, and strictly for the connoisseur. Recently a new 'wonder' material has been introduced under the trade name Goretex. The material is a laminate of three layers of which the middle one is PTFE. Because the PTFE layer is permeable to air but impermeable to water, it has been possible to make garments which are both waterproof yet condensation free. However, since all the cloth for the garments is imported, and together with expensive welding techniques at the make-up stage, this has meant that the retail price of the simplest of these garments is approaching £40. Better to spend the money on other forms of protection!

These remarks about materials for cagoules or jackets apply equally to overtrousers. Except for Alpine rock climbing or the more remote climbing areas of Britain, these can hardly be considered as essential, but caught out on a wet day on Scafell they become surprisingly desirable.

Trousers and Breeches

'Das Bluejeans' is the name given to British climbers by the Germans, with some truth, for nowhere has the cult of denim been stronger than amongst rock climbers here. For purely rock climbing purposes, jeans are perfectly adequate; many climbers wear them all the time, even on high mountain crags though against all the warnings of the mountain safety pundits.

Yet there can be little doubt that breeches are more suited to all aspects of mountain sport, and that includes rock climbing. They are made in a variety of materials, the woollen ones such as Derby tweed or Bonneville tweed being more suited to winter use, while cotton fabrics such as mole cord and corduroy can be used all year round. A recent development is the use of stretch Helanca fabric, which is proving popular if expensive. Breeches should be cut so that it is possible to raise the knees really high without experiencing that drag on knees and thighs which is such a drawback with tight-fitting jeans. They should also have a double seat to protect against wear and cold, and some well-made types have side pockets with zip closures. The hardest wearing material is molecord, the smartest Helanca, the best value Derby tweed. Whipcord is to be avoided!

Thermal Wear

Few items have taken the climbing world by such a storm as that created by fibre pile clothing. Whereas a few short years ago the Norwegian oiled wool sweater was the climber's favourite shield against the cold, it is now unusual to see climbers wearing any knitted garment which is not nylon fibre pile.

Originally designed as underwear for North Sea divers, the material is basically knitted nylon backing with a furry pile, about 8 mm in length, woven into the backing. Inferior materials have the pile stuck onto the backing rather than woven into it. One of the great beauties of fibre pile as far as the climber is concerned, is that it is almost indestructible. Although marginally dearer than wool, it will far outlast the natural fibre. Its other

Rapidly becoming the most sought after material is Helanca, from which ski trousers are made. It is elasticated and, because of the high content of nylon, very hard-wearing. It is also the most expensive.

Cotton corduroy is comfortable and warm, at least when dry.

One of the most popular materials for breeches is Derby Tweed. Although difficult to find in pure wool nowadays, this 70/30 mixture ensures warmth even when wet, which makes for a four-season garment. Derby Tweed is one of the cheaper materials.

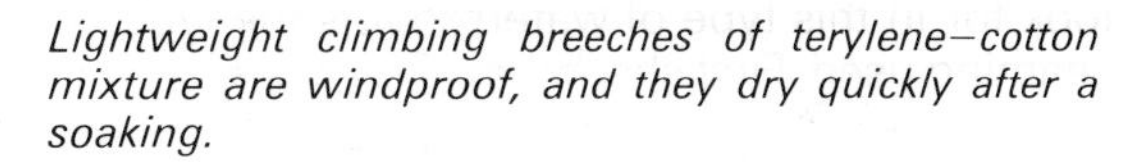

Lightweight climbing breeches of terylene–cotton mixture are windproof, and they dry quickly after a soaking.

Just about universally worn by climbers is the fibre-pile or polar jacket, made from 100 per cent nylon. Light, warm and very hard wearing, they also have the advantage of drying quickly. This one is the Helly-Hansen polar jacket. Helly fibre-pile is woven in a special way with the pile wrapped twice around the backing material, and is undoubtedly the best.

The North Cape 'Ogre' jacket. Another popular fibre-pile garment. That shown has a beefy zip and pockets; this type of fibre-pile is also woven, unlike some of the cheaper types on the market where the pile is bonded to the backing material.

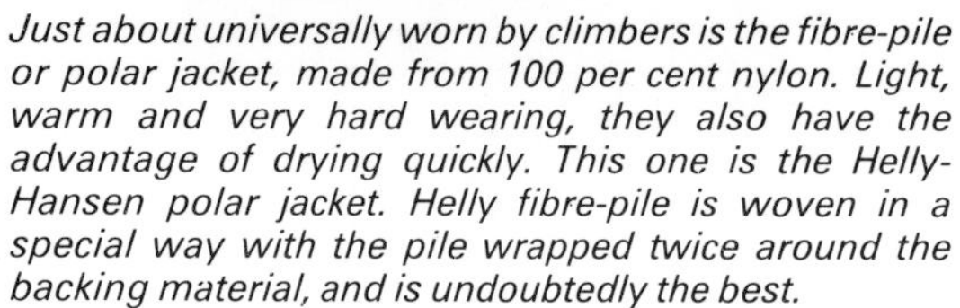

Some form of glove is essential where older forms of belay technique are in use. They should be of natural fibre rather than nylon which can melt, and there should be no gap between wrist and sleeve. These are Millarmitts.

good points are its light weight, and its ability to dry very quickly after a soaking.

Perhaps the best-known make is Helly Hansen, whose fibre pile material is still regarded as top. The Aberdeen firm of North Cape also make several popular garments. Fibre pile trousers, originally intended as underwear, and excellent for that purpose in very cold places, are being increasingly used as outer garments for rock climbing. The natural stretch of fibre pile garments combined with their light weight, warmth and durability, make them ideal for rock climbing.

Rucksacks

Almost any old bag will suffice to carry protection slings, rock boots and a spare sweater the half-mile or so from road to crag, and that is all that is necessary for most rock climbing. But a rock

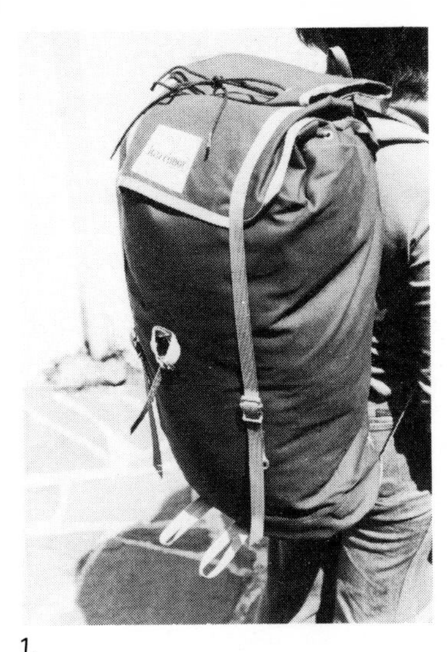

1.

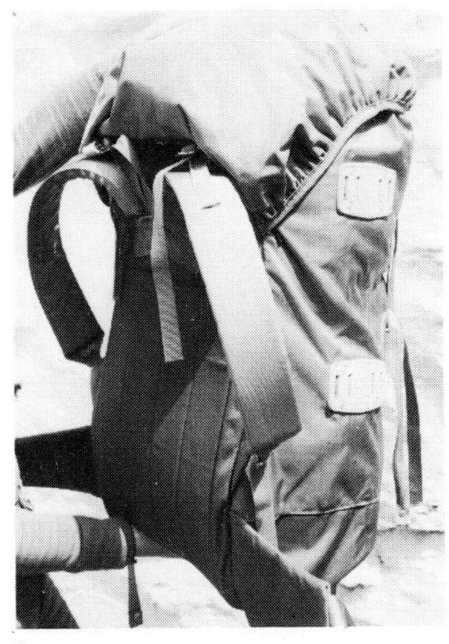

2.

3.

1. *Karrimor 'Chamonix', an inexpensive sack of relatively large (45 litres) capacity. This one is probably large enough to carry basic camping gear, or else bivouac equipment for an Alpine rock climb. It is made in canvas only.*

2. *Berghaus Cyclops Sack, designed on the so-called 'ergonomic' principle. It has a simple internal frame which can be bent to fit the wearer's back and so ensure a comfortable fit.*

3. *Day sack or 'butty bag'. This one is the Karrimor 'Pinnacle', and is a popular basic rucksack with rock climbers. It has a capacity of 28 litres, and is available in canvas or nylon. The two loops are intended as ice axe carriers.*

4. *Haston Vallot. A typical modern climbing sack of 70 litres capacity. It has two pockets in the top flap, one of them accessible behind the wearer's head. The leather side patches can be fitted with 'scotch' pockets to increase capacity; the straps provided will carry skis.*

5. *Haston Vallot. The comfortable, padded canvas back contributes to a good 'carry', as do the soft shoulder straps. A hip belt takes some of the weight from the climber's shoulders when humping a lot of gear, but is not usually used when climbing. The webbing loop above the shoulder straps is intended for sack hauling (where the climbing is too dfficult to carry a sack) though this will wear a rucksack out more quickly than any other climbing activity, short of actually dropping it!*

6. *Famous French rucksack, the Millet model Sherpa features an abrasion-resistant leather base. As with any form of backpacking, it pays to carry heavy objects low down and close to the back.*

4.

5.

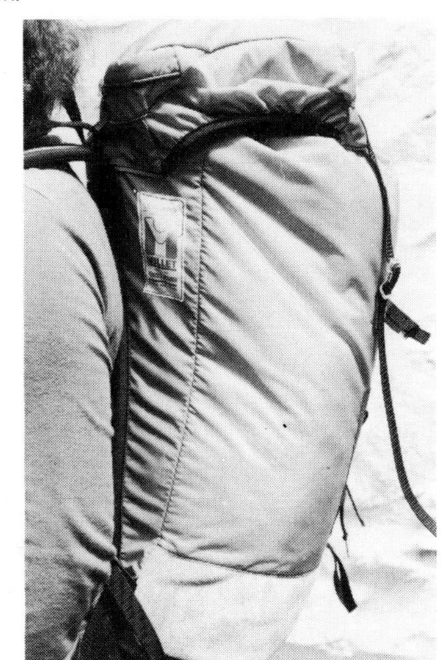

6.

climber might soon find himself carrying camping gear many miles over Scottish bogs, humping equipment up to an Alpine hut, or even carrying in or on his sack all the accoutrements of the ice climber complete with a pair of skis! So it pays the beginner to give a little attention to what he thinks he might be doing in his first couple of years as a climber, and buying a rucksack on that basis.

Traditionally, a climbing sack is a single compartment sack of tall and narrow proportions, with a reinforced base to cope with inevitable abrasion. In use on a climb, the narrow shape offers the least obstruction to upward movement, but since the narrowness confers lack of capacity for the secondary purpose of load carrying, most modern climbing sacks have detachable external pockets and also extendible main compartments. Thus they can be used to haul big loads to high huts or camps, and can then be reduced in size for the actual climb.

Capacity needs to be decided. For use as a day sack, where you might need a spare sweater, food, and those lightweight waterproofs, 25 litres will suffice. If camping gear (i.e. tentage, sleeping bag and cooking equipment) is added, then 70 litres would not be too much. For those carrying several days' provisions plus camping plus mountain gear up to a mountain hut, the biggest capacity sacks are required—about 90 litres. Even then, ruthless pruning of equipment is necessary.

Then decide on material, and there is a choice between canvas or nylon. There is little difference in price between the two, but nylon has the advantage of light weight and greater strength, and its waterproof qualities are superior when new. Canvas is heavier when dry, and much heavier when wet when it becomes stiff as a board and can freeze. It is rather more resistant to abrasion, and its waterproof qualities are more consistent throughout its life than nylon. In spite of its apparent disadvantages, there is a resurgence of interest in canvas, as is evidenced by the increasing variety of rucksacks becoming available in this material. Coming on to the market is a new material, textured nylon (Fe 100), which has waterproof qualities superior to canvas and nylon, but with the appearance of canvas.

There has recently been some effort made by rucksack designers to increase the comfort or 'carry' of climbing sacks. Various anatomic designs are now available, most of them featuring shaped and padded backs with rudimentary internal frames which can be altered to fit the wearer. They often have some form of padded hip belt whose function is to transfer load from shoulders to pelvis. Although these latest generation rucksacks are outstandingly comfortable in use, they have inevitably become expensive, and it will pay the prospective purchaser to examine some of the older designs before making a choice to suit his or her particular needs.

Free Climbing Techniques

The rock climber is essentially concerned with using a combination of techniques to climb a difficult route up a cliff which might be twenty feet, or four thousand feet, high. The use of ropes, slings and other protection to safeguard life is an entirely different consideration from the means by which the climb is made; these items are not intended to be for direct aid but are for protection only.

Free climbing is climbing by your own strength and agility, using your judgement to overcome the problems before you. Sometimes it will be necessary to use pegs or protection slings for direct aid, and the aid allowed on a climb is always stated in the Guide Book route description. A competent climber will need to develop skills in a variety of techniques.

Balance Climbing

Essentially, this is the ability to move up the rock face on footholds rather than by using the arms to pull upwards. A climber is said to be balance climbing when he is moving with no handholds available, and so using the hands for guidance rather than to gain support, such as when traversing a ledge where the wall above leans outward, tending to push him off. It is fundamentally important that the body is kept upright, avoiding the natural inclination to hug the rock. Standing upright 'in balance' aids agility and improves upward vision; it also reduces the tendency for the toes to be pushed backwards off the rock.

Steep, open climbing: Bovine, VS, on Clogwyn y Wenallt. Good stylists keep three limbs in contact with the rock at all times, moving only one limb at once.

Opposite:
Balance Climbing. The leader here has very little in the way of handholds as he moves up in balance. He is careful to keep his feet horizontal, and his toes are on the extreme edge of the foot ledge which effectively extends his platform, enabling him to keep in balance.

Right:
It is important to stand upright, avoiding the tendency to hug the rock. This keeps the climber's centre of gravity over his feet which lessens the likelihood of his boots thrusting backwards off the footholds.

Friction Climbing

Many routes involve climbing up rock slabs of varying angles of steepness, some of which will have neither handholds nor footholds. The only way of getting up these is by friction climbing. Here the modern rock boot comes into its own with its cling rubber sole which bends to grip the rock. Friction climbing calls for pressure holds made by the hands; in doing this the climber's arm is reversed so that the ball of the hand, with the fingers pointing downwards, presses on to the rock. Thus, using toe friction and pressure holds, the climber is able to 'pad' up blank slabs. Rhythm is particularly important in friction climbing; it is essential that upward momentum is maintained since this reduces the amount of friction required to a marked degree.

When friction climbing on wet rock, rubber-soled boots of any sort tend to slip, since the rock surface becomes greasy. This can be overcome to some extent by wearing old socks over your rock boots. The thicker, felted sock is much better than the thin nylon variety. But this is a desperate expedient, because the socks last no time at all before wearing through at the toes! Another advantage in wet conditions is to wear woollen or molecord breeches, since they provide a surprising amount of friction.

Hand Jamming

The ability to hand jam is very important to the modern rock climber, since many modern climbs would be impossible without competent use of this technique. Cracks in the rock are climbed on most routes, and the least strenuous way is by placing the hand into the crack, and using the opposition of fingers and knuckles to provide a secure handhold. Obviously cracks occur in different widths, and it is sometimes possible to slot the whole hand in so that the ball of the hand acts as a wedge. At other times only the first two finger joints will fit and the thumb must be utilized

Good handholds, in climbing parlance 'jug handles', or 'Thank God' holds.

on the outside of the crack to give the necessary opposition. Where the whole hand will fit into the crack, a more secure jam results if the thumb is crossed on the palm rather than used in line with the fingers. Often a better jam is obtained if the hand is placed upside down, i.e. with the thumb beneath, though this makes it difficult to move upwards since the elbow joint is now the wrong way round.

With wider cracks it is possible to jam the clenched fist, by making use of the fist's tendency to expand when clenched, which provides the

Friction Climbing. The flexible sole of the rock boot is really at home when climbing slabs such as this. The climber must take advantage of every ripple in the rock surface to gain height; here his left hand is reversed in a pressure hold.

Left *Hand jamming is an important rock climbing technique; here the thumb has been placed across the palm to give the hand more mass. All hand jamming methods are unkind to skin!*

Right *Finger jam in a narrow crack. The thumb pushes in opposition to the fingers.*

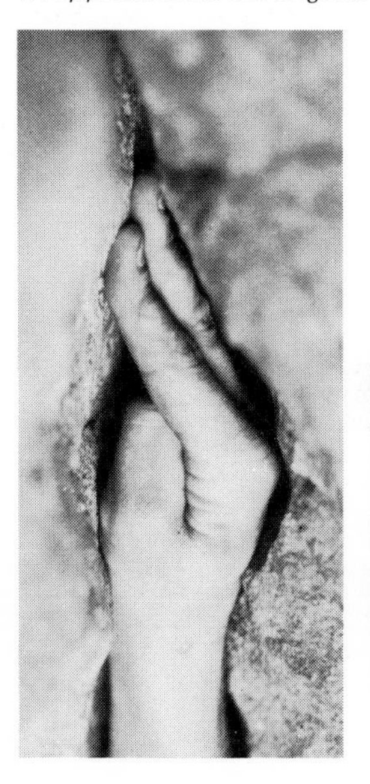

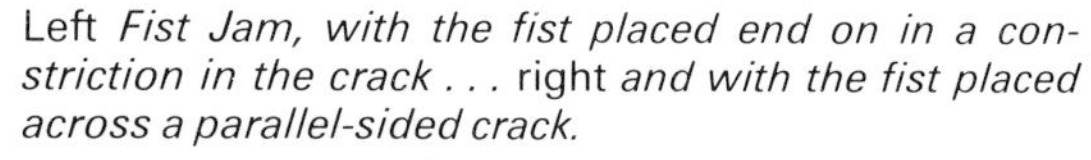

Left *Fist Jam, with the fist placed end on in a constriction in the crack . . .* right *and with the fist placed across a parallel-sided crack.*

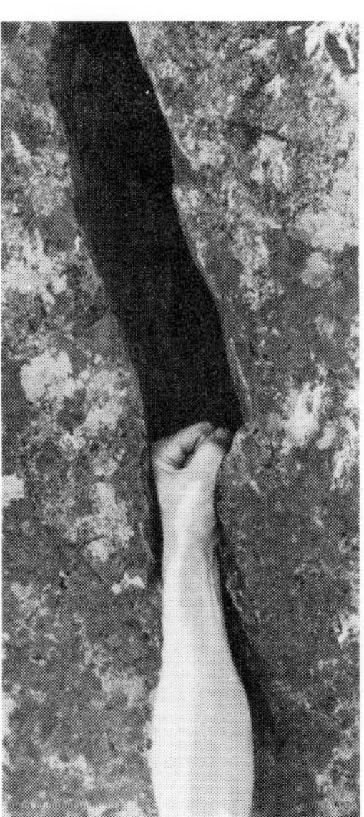

An Extreme grade hand jamming crack. The Neb Direct finish at Tremadoc (photo: David Lancely).

Laybacking. The climber leans back from the crack, his arms being called on to take all the thrust of his legs. A strenuous method of climbing, and one where it pays the climber to move quickly if he is to conserve energy.

jamming action. But fist jams usually feel less secure than other types of jam.

Where the crack is deep enough, it is sometimes possible to jam the whole arm; this is often a good idea when resting before a strenuous section.

Toe jamming is commonly used in narrow cracks, though you should never put your foot into a crack beyond the broad part of the toe—your foot might stick when you attempt to move upwards! The reason for the friction rand on rock boots is to aid toe jamming.

Laybacking

Where two rock faces meet at an approximate right angle, they form a corner or dièdre (dihedral in America). A clean-cut crack is often found in this corner, and it is possible to ascend by walking the feet up one wall, moving the hands up the crack at the same time. Hands and feet will need to be nearly at the same level to prevent the feet from sliding off; thus the whole thrust of the legs, as well as most of the body weight, is on the climber's hands—a most strenuous way of climbing. This can be a rapid and elegant means of ascent for a competent climber, but there are a number of pitfalls for the unwary. Because the method is tiring, it is almost impossible to attach any protection, and any attempt to do so is likely to end in failure or even a fall. It is often difficult to judge just how strenuous a particular crack is going to be, when factors such as greasy rock or a deteriorating crack might not be obvious viewed from below.

Where the layback has become too difficult to continue, the climber is faced with attempting to transform it into a jam, a tricky transition. There are few pure laybacks to be found on British rock because the ancient granites usually have weathered rugosities (wrinkles), which provide a welcome toe-hold here and there for the tiring leader. Younger rocks found in Europe and the USA have long layback cracks, which are usually

A layaway move, similar in principle to a layback but using side pull handholds rather than the (more obvious) layback crack.

rough, clean and dry as well as sharp-edged, which makes laybacking easier.

Layaway

If a climber encounters a series of vertical holds, or small cracks, on a climb where there are no convenient horizontal holds, he might be able to place a foot on a high vertical hold and, using a side-pull handhold, lay away from the foothold to gain height in a similar manner to a layback. This technique is commonly used, but often for single moves only.

Undercling

Where a large flake, or overlap, of rock offers a sharp edge of rock pointing downwards, it is possible to lean out and use the edge for the hands, while walking the feet along high up, just below the hands in much the same manner as a layback. This is known as an undercling, and is most useful when traversing.

Bridging

Whereas our feet carry our weight for a whole day without much complaint, our hands are much less strong. It is of great advantage when climbing if the feet can be organized to do the load carrying. In fact, it is often possible when climbing a steep crack, or corner or groove, to leave aside strenuous jamming and bridge out with one foot on each side wall, so standing in balance. Many steep corners can be climbed entirely by this method, with big conserving of energy.

Chimneying

A crack becomes a chimney in rock climbing when it becomes wide enough to admit the climber's body. Cracks which are too big to fist jam, and too narrow to get into, are called off-width cracks. Chimneys are climbed by the back and foot method, where the climber's back and hands are on one wall of the chimney and his feet on the other. Upward progress is made by placing the palms of the hands (and sometimes one foot)

Bridging. The climber here is able to stand in balance by putting his foot out on to the right wall, and in this way he is able to rest before attempting the next couple of moves—the crux of this climb. The route is one of the favourite old Very Severes, 'Lion', on Carreg Wastad.

When chimneying, the back is placed on one wall and the feet are placed on the other. It is one of the easiest and safest methods of climbing since it is possible to rest at any time . . .

. . . however, when the chimney becomes as narrow as this one, progress is more strenuous, and it will be found easier to climb on the outside of the crack if holds can be found.

on the wall behind him, and pushing up. The back is then rested on the wall, and the feet brought up opposite until the move can be repeated. It is an easy and safe technique to use and, of course, the climber can rest at any time. If the chimney becomes constricted more effort might be required, but if anything this technique feels safer. Where the chimney widens out to something greater than can be back-and-footed, bridging techniques have to be used; when too wide for bridging, then one or other of the walls will have to be climbed by whatever method is possible.

Hand Traverse

Sometimes a good horizontal crack offers a means of traversing by handhold, though the rock beneath is devoid of footholds. In this case there is nothing for it but to swarm along the crack hand over hand. Speed and confidence are the key, and it certainly helps if the toes obtain whatever grip they can on the rock below. Progress is much quicker if the hands leap-frog one another along the crack. The placing of runners must be very quick if at all, since the muscular effort of hanging on while placing the runner, might so fatigue the climber that he falls off further along! Or else he must rest 'illegally' on the runner he has so painstakingly placed.

Tension Traverse

A natural crack line sometimes peters out in the middle of a face, and an alternative crack appears a little way off. If the area between the two lines has no climbable weakness, it has to be crossed by tension traverse. Here, the lead climber lays

A frequent move in rock climbing: the mantelshelf. Used for getting on to a ledge, it requires turning a pull-up into a press-up and then stepping up alongside the hands. It is considered bad form to use your knees.

Hand traversing: moving across the rock with good handholds but nothing for the feet. It is always better to keep the feet on the rock as here. This rock is sandstone at Helsby in Cheshire.

away on tension from his main ropes using friction or vertical rugosities for holds. His main ropes are fed via a high runner, usually much higher than himself to give him diagonal support; he may choose to control the tension rope himself or let his second do it.

Pendulum

Rather than manoeuvre across blank rock on tension, a pendulum might be set up. A high runner is threaded and the climber descends a distance greater than that which he hopes to traverse. He then runs backwards and forwards across the face until he can work up enough momentum to reach the new line!

Routes with big pendulums on them are often inescapable as the only way of getting off is by going upwards.

Protection Techniques

The whole philosophy of protection technique in climbing is associated with the belay, and belaying methods. 'Belay' is an old seaman's term for a point where a rope can be made fast; thus a climber's belay is a place where the climber can secure himself to the rock. By holding the main ropes around his body, the climber can safeguard his partner in the event of a fall. Knowing how to belay safely is of utmost importance. It requires great concentration on the part of the belayer, and, particularly when holding a leader fall, resolute action.

Belaying

When the climber reaches the stance at the end of a pitch, his method of attachment to the belay will depend upon what is available as an anchor, and also to some extent on the belaying technique to be used. The anchor point might be a spike of rock, a nutsling, a threaded sling, or a natural chockstone (a pebble wedged in a crack). An alternative would be to use a peg, which will often be found *in situ*. Ideally, two anchor points should be used, one of them being capable of resisting a pull from any direction. They should be above the waist level of the belayer so that he remains in an upright position and is thus better able to control the ropes in the event of a fall. It is usual for the main ropes to link the belayer to the anchor slings, each rope leading from the attachment point at the waist through the karabiner on the anchor sling and back to the waist. The anchor sling is tied off to a karabiner, or threaded through the main ropes (in the case of a direct tie-on) and made fast with half hitches. This method of belay attachment offers easy adjustment.

Ideas about holding falls have changed somewhat in the last couple of years. There is now a more general appreciation of the very high

Sticht Plates. These are available for every combination of rope size in use. Illustrated are 9/II-mm and double 9 mm plates, with and without spring. These particular examples show faulty quality control since all have bad burrs in the slots. As with everything else, inspect carefully what you are buying.

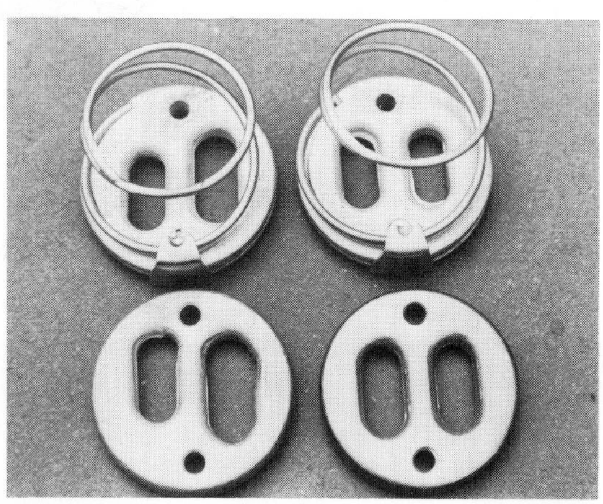

In use, the spring prevents the karabiner riding up against the Sticht plate and jamming the rope accidentally. Here, a single 11-mm rope is being used in the correct slot in a 9/II-mm plate. It would be asking for trouble to use this plate for double 9-mm ropes, since there would be considerable loss of friction on the larger slot.

Bringing up a second using a waist belay. The leader is on a fairly typical stance and has a belay well above waist level which would prevent him from being dragged downwards, and another below his left elbow (a nut sling) which will guard against an upward pull when the second leads through. His left hand is the control hand which will be called upon to provide friction if the second falls; this is gloved to prevent rope burns.

forces involved in stopping a falling leader, and many climbers now use automatic fall arrest devices such as the Sticht plate. There are really four methods of belaying to consider.

Waist Belay. This is a time-honoured method, very widely used both in Britain and the United States. It is a so-called 'dynamic' belay, which simply means that the belayer's body stops the fall and the belay stops *him* being dragged from his stance. Thus a cushioning effect is achieved.

The main ropes are held around the belayer's back at waist level, the braking effect being achieved by friction around his waist. His controlling hand is the one furthest from the person climbing, and the amount of control is increased by wrapping the rope around the wrist. If a fall occurs, the belayer progressively increases the braking effect by bringing his control hand in front of his body, which makes the friction greater. Although commonly used, this method of belaying still leaves much to be desired.

It is a well-known fact that nylon ropes have a low melting point. However, it is usual when using a waist belay for the main ropes to be held *over* the belayer's anchor ropes behind his back, increasing the risk of these melting from the great amount of friction generated in a severe fall. For many years this danger has been recognized, and climbers have been advised to hold the main ropes under the anchor ropes, but the advice has been ignored. The reason is that many climbers feel there to be a real chance of the ropes being snatched completely away from the belayer if the leader should fall before he has placed a runner, so that he falls directly on to the belay. Perhaps the real reason that the waist belay continues to be used at all is because climbers feel that the possibility of a severe leader fall is so remote that the risk is acceptable. One thing is certain about waist belays: the belayer must wear gloves to

A real danger with waist belay methods is the belayer's anchor rope being melted by the friction of the main ropes in the event of a fall. The oft-quoted alternative—holding the main ropes beneath the climber's anchor rope—leaves the belayer with the prospect of having the ropes snatched completely away beneath him if the leader falls without having put a runner on.

As the second leads through to become the new leader, the belayer must hold the main ropes around his waist in such a manner that if the leader should fall, he will do so on the opposite side of the belayer's body to the control hand. This means that it is sometimes necessary for the belayer to change the direction of the main ropes around his waist and, of course, change the control hand too. This would happen if the leader were to traverse to the left from his position in this picture, so that he was climbing in a position to the left of a vertical line above the belay. Note how the belayer here ensures that no twist in the rope is allowed to pass by feeding the ropes through his fingers.

protect hands and wrists from rope-burn, and he should also protect his arms.

Sticht plate belay, dynamic. The sticht plate, in common with a number of a similar devices, is designed to do in a mechanical way what the waist belay does using the belayer's body: apply a controlled braking force to the main rope to stop a falling climber. Because it is designed with some precision, its effect can be finely calculated, and because of the way it is used it is less dependent on positive action from the belayer.

It consists simply of a light alloy plate in which are cut one or two slots, depending on the number of ropes used. The ropes are simply pushed through the slots in two bights, and a single karabiner clipped through them. In use as a dynamic belay the karabiner is clipped to the harness of the belayer, who, of course, is anchored to the rock. In normal climbing use, the ropes can be easily fed through one slot, past the karabiner, and out through the same slot. But if a fall occurs, the loading of the rope causes the plate to ride up against the karabiner causing a lot of friction, automatically applying a brake. The belayer is only required to apply normal instinctive pressure on the control rope; a braking force of 475 lbs can be achieved. If the braking force needs to be increased, the rope should be passed around two karabiners behind the plate instead of one, when the braking effort is about 880 lbs. In addition, the main ropes can be passed around the belayer's body if more friction is desired. Later models of sticht plate are fitted with a spring which prevents the karabiner jamming the ropes accidentally. Use of these devices is not recommended with three-strand twisted ropes, only with braided sheath ropes.

Sticht plate belay. This clearly shows the action of the spring which is designed to hold the karabiner away from the plate to avoid accidental braking. The small cord prevents the plate from dropping too far down the rope away from the karabiner.

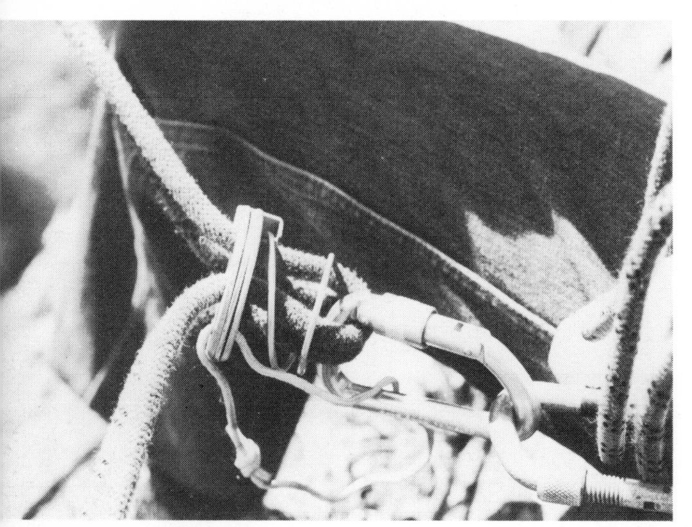

Sticht plate belay, direct. Where a heavy leader is being belayed by a person of slight build, it might be preferable to handle the leader ropes directly from an anchor rather than from the belayer's harness. In this way the stress of the fall should be borne by the anchor instead of the belayer's body. If this method is used, the belayer should have a separate and secure anchor, and the main

The Sticht plate belay in action, the best of the modern methods, requiring from the belayer only normal instinctive reaction to stop a fall. The prospect of holding a falling leader using the older waist belay methods might be so daunting that action from the belayer could be delayed, if only for a split second; this could mean the difference between life and death to the leader. Using a belay brake eliminates this danger.

If more friction is required, two karabiners can be used behind the spring instead of one, or the main ropes can be taken around the waist to the control hand as shown here.

The Sticht plate can be used to belay directly from a peg as here. This method is not so popular in Britain as the dynamic technique described above; note that the belayer must have an independent belay. The short cord which can be seen on the plate, linking it to the karabiner, prevents the plate from dropping down the ropes.

Munter Hitch. This is a very effective braking method, though rather hard on the rope. Where two ropes are used, each should have its own karabiner. Any karabiner used in belay work should have a screw keeper on the gate to prevent accidental opening, and it is only sensible to learn to clip live ropes such as these into the karabiners in such a way that they will not unscrew the keepers as they are drawn through.

This is the shoulder belay, which was the standard method of holding a rope until about 15 years ago. It is still used by some leaders to bring up lightweight seconds, but any attempt to hold a falling leader will result in a broken collar bone for the belayer, who is likely to let go of the ropes altogether!

Used in this way the hitch is a most effective fall arrest device, relying on the friction of the rope running over itself for its braking power. Its great disadvantage is that a severe fall is likely to damage the sheath of the rope beyond further use. Where double ropes are in use, separate hitches should be used on two karabiners.

Running Belays

All running belays are used in the same way. A sling is attached to the rock by one method or another, and the main rope is clipped to the sling by a karabiner. The main rope is then free to run, but, should a fall occur, the leader will fall only as far as the runner, instead of as far as the belay, which might be a long way below.

It seems only a few short years ago that a climber's runners would consist of a couple of long spliced slings with those appalling ex War Dept. karabiners! Today's climber carries about twenty slings, of which the majority are short slings threaded on to nuts of bewildering variety.

Plain slings. In its simplest form, a runner is slipped onto a natural spike of rock as the leader climbs past it, and the main rope is clipped into the karabiner carried by the sling. Plain slings (those without nuts) are used for this purpose and several of these are carried, a variety of rope and

rope anchor must be capable of withstanding loads from any direction (incidentally, a criterion which few belays fulfil).

Munter hitch. This is an interesting application which is finding a lot of favour among Continental climbers. It consists quite simply of half a clove hitch made with the main rope on the karabiner attached to the belay anchor, whether the anchor is the climber's harness or a direct one attached to the rock.

Opposite:
Wherever possible, two belay anchors should be used. Here, a sling placed round a natural thread is backed up by a sound nut sling. The ends of the main ropes have been used to extend the belays so that the second has a comfortable stance. The main ropes have been kept separated and will run out easily without getting into a tangle. The waist belay is being used and the second, Helen Brown, is wisely wearing gloves.

Plain sling used double on a spike of rock as a runner. This is an 3-foot length of 9-mm rope fastened with a double fisherman's knot.

Thread runner on 1-inch supertape. The ends of the sling must both be brought back to the karabiner.

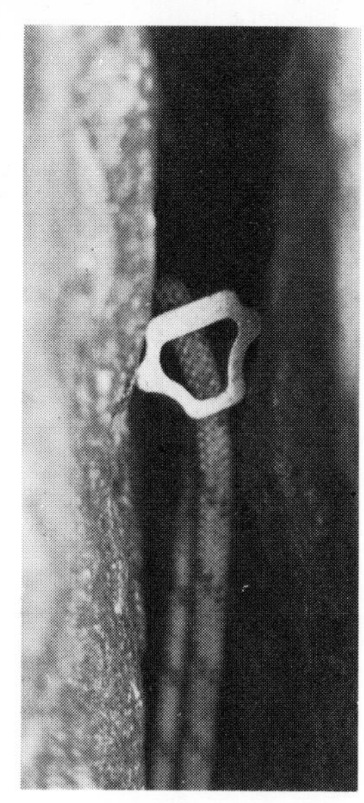

Moac wedge nut runner in a good placement (left) . . . and (right) another first class nut. This is a 'Cog'; any downward loading will twist the nut which will tighten its grip on the rock.

tapes according to individual preference. Different lengths of plain slings are required. Long ones are often handy for use when belaying on large rock spikes. Where a spike runner with a rounded top is encountered, a long tape sling will be much less inclined to lift off as the leader moves above. It is one of the more galling feelings in life to see a sorely needed runner slide off down the rope when you are in no position to reverse and replace it! If a long tape sling still looks as if it will lift, weigh it down with a couple of karabiners.

Plain slings are also needed for that most satisfying of all runners—the thread. A small diameter sling of 5 or 6 mm will sometimes be a godsend as a thread runner, while many climbers carry a piece of 4-mm 'bootlace' just for emergencies. Whilst not strong enough to hold a fall, it can be used to lower a desperate leader. Long slings are also needed sometimes to extend a short runner to improve the line of the main rope. If a good short nut runner is placed just under an overhang, for instance, a main rope clipped directly to it will bind against the rock as the leader moves up causing a lot of unwelcome rope drag; a long sling extending the runner allows the main rope to clear the rock.

Where a sling is threaded, whether around a natural chockstone or through a hole in the rock, the karabiner should be clipped through both ends of the sling; the other method, of threading the sling through its own bight, should be regarded as dangerous since the sudden load of a fall will cause the bight to slide up the sling, and will possibly melt the bight.

Nut slings. Without doubt, the device which has revolutionized protection in recent years is the nut. Designs have developed from the simple hexagonal shape of the early types, the most popular ones being the American Chouinard wedges (stoppers) and hexagonals (hexentrics). Techniques of placement of nuts are fairly straightforward—they are simply slotted into a convenient crack until they jam. It takes a bit of practice to develop an eye for placement; the ideal cracks are wider on the inside than outside and which are constricted to prevent the nut from dropping too far down. However, satisfactory placement can be obtained in parallel side cracks with nuts such as the hexentric or cog, which are

Opposite:
When climbing with doubled ropes, it is important that the leader pays attention to the lead of his ropes through the runners. The ropes must lead out in as straight a line as possible, and should never be crossed, otherwise excessive rope drag will result. The climb is 'The Pause' on the Etive Slabs near Glencoe, and the climber Paul Nunn. It is graded Hard VS.

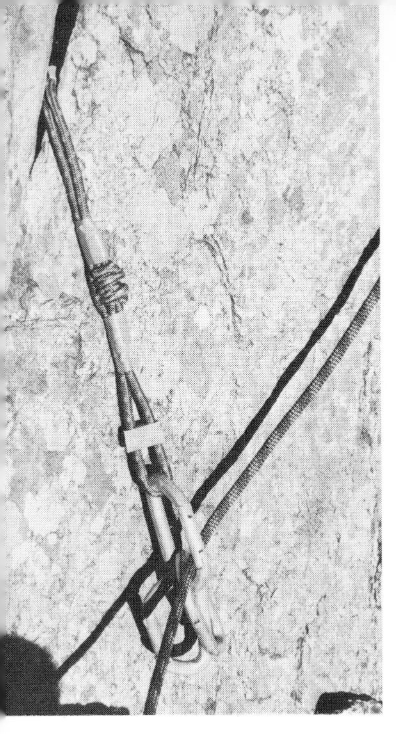

Left *Two nuts can be put on a single sling to advantage, since it increases the choice of placement for the climber; where this is done the lower nut should be slid out of the bight of the sling and the karabiner clipped in below it. If the nut looks as if it might lift out with the upward drag of the rope, the sling can be weighted down as here, or else extended with another sling.*

Centre *'Friends' offer a mechanical improvement on ordinary nuts. Loading opens out the cams to increase their grip, while their rapid placement means that extremely difficult routes can be climbed 'free'* *(see page 65).*

Right *Another mechanical camming device, the 'cam lok'. These are really designed for parallel-sided cracks, though of course they work very well in the more weathered type of rocks found in Britain.*

The runner in the right corner has been extended to reduce rope drag, but a longer sling would be more effective.

designed to 'cam' when loaded. Sometimes it is possible to place two nuts in opposite directions so that one prevents the other from lifting out of a delicate placement.

Where smaller nuts are involved, these are often to be found with a ready-made wire sling swaged on. A short tape sling is usually used to prevent the wire sling from lifting, and where this is so, a karabiner should be interposed between wire and tape, since the small radius of the wire will greatly reduce the breaking strain of the tape.

Nuts are made from a soft grade of aluminium which means that they grip the rock when placed. It is not necessary for the leader to snatch the sling downwards to jam the nut when the placement has been made. The second will have great difficulty in removing the runner if this is done (witness the amount of expensive aluminium ware to be found abandoned on the rock climbs of Britain today).

Peg runners. These are sometimes found on rock climbs, though not so many since the advent of nuts. They will appear in the description of the climb if they are legitmate; if a peg is described, but is not found *in situ*, then you are entitled to put one in. Protection pegs should not be used for aid, but it is quite permissible to use aid pegs for protection.

Protection layout. It is important that the leader thinks about the layout of his protection as he climbs. If climbing on single rope there is little he can do to minimize rope drag at the runners, beyond extending the really bad ones in order to keep his rope in as straight a line as possible. With double ropes, however, he has a much greater chance of keeping his ropes straight no matter how much the climb zig-zags, and when he finishes the pitch the two ropes should follow independent lines of runners without crossing.

Protecting traverses. If a traverse is involved, the leader must also consider the safety of his second. If the pitch finishes at a belay much higher than the traverse, then the leader had best keep one of his two ropes free from runners so that it can lead diagonally upwards from the second as he starts the traverse. If, on the other hand, the pitch ends on the same level or below that of the second, then the only way to protect him is by use of a backrope. In this case, one of the two ropes is left on a suitable runner on the belay which the second is leaving, and the leader pays out on this back rope while taking in on the other. Thus the second is supported at each side, and in the event of a fall is not faced with the prospect of a horrendous pendulum with a possible smash into the rock. The runner supporting the back rope, will, it is hoped, flick off when required!

Climber Ray Jardine is finger jamming under this impressive roof, protected by 'Friends'. The climb is Separate Reality in Yosemite, graded 5.12a (photo: John Lakey).

Descent Technique: Abseiling

Of all techniques used in rock climbing, abseiling is at the same time the most exhilarating, and the most dangerous. Over the years many famous climbers of vast experience have met their deaths in accidents associated with abseiling. Utmost care must be taken at all stages of abseiling. Beginners should practice the technique on small, safe rock walls, protected from above by a competent climber holding them on a safety rope.

With most rock climbs, and even the great rock routes of the Alps, having completed the climb the climbers are able to walk off the back of the crag or mountain by a comparatively easy route. Generally speaking, climbing down rock climbs is not practised, since it is much more difficult than climbing up. Sometimes, however, it is unavoidable—on sea stacks such as the Old Man of Hoy or, simply, if you cannot complete the ascent. In order to make a descent, climbers use a controlled slide down the doubled main ropes, the abseil. In some areas such as the Dolomites, it is not unusual to make a dozen abseils in succession to get off a mountain.

The abseil point. It will be quite obvious to anyone about to embark on an abseil that his life will depend on his point of anchor, so he must be sure that this anchor is absolutely safe. Climbers ideally like to abseil from well-rounded natural projections of rock, so that the ropes will pull down without snagging afterwards. However, it is quite common to abseil from a peg or a natural chockstone. In this case the main ropes are threaded through a rope sling and can be easily retrieved, though the sling itself has to be sacrificed. Some pegs have a steel ring attachment specially for this purpose.

Setting up the abseil. While the main ropes are being used for descending, it follows that something else has to be used for belaying purposes. Rather than risk a slip from the belay ledge, both climbers should attach themselves to the anchor point with a suitable sling. If a single length of rope is being used for the abseil, one end is threaded through the ring of the peg belay, or through the rope sling. If the belay point is a rock spike, the rope middle is simply positioned over it.

However, the usual practice now is to use two ropes, and knot them at the belay with a double fisherman's knot, after threading the end of one through the peg or sling, if used.

As with every aspect of abseiling, it pays to be most careful. It is easy enough to make a mistake in rigging the ropes and then watch one, or even both, disappear down the mountain.

After knotting, the ropes are thrown down in the direction of descent. They should first be coiled (a small diameter coil is best for a direct aim, particularly when there is a strong up-

'That may not have been the first descent, but I bet it was the quickest.'

The abseil anchor might be a suitable rock spike as here: often the ropes can be drawn down quite easily from a smooth and rounded belay. It is important to remember which colour rope to pull to avoid trying to drag the knot behind the belay spike; if the wrong rope is pulled, it is likely to snag in both directions. If there is any doubt about retrieving the rope, it is better to place a sling around the belay and thread the ropes through it. The sling, of course, has to be sacrificed. Climbers on Alpine routes often carry a length of old rope to cut up to make abseil slings.

The Dulfer, or classic abseil. Now little used, it is as well to know how it is done if only because no equipment is required.

draught). It is unusual for the ropes to fall without any snagging: the climbers must judge whether the first man down will be able to sort out the tangle. It also helps if the rope ends are fastened together, which further stops the climber from abseiling right off the ropes! If there is doubt about the first man down being able to clear any snag, the ropes will have to be hauled up and another attempt made.

Retrieving the rope. Once the descent is made, the climbers haul on one end of the rope (having unknotted the lower ends), pulling it through the belay above. The whole process is then repeated.

Where two ropes are knotted at the belay, it is important to make a mental note when tying the knot of which colour rope to pull, otherwise the knot will snag on the sling or peg ring. If the ropes fall across the edge of the stance (which often happens), make sure that the knot lies below the ledge so that it won't snag there.

Even if the ropes appear to be hauling down in a satisfactory way, care should be taken. They can be hauled down quickly until the weight of the upwards travelling rope lessens. They must then be hauled more slowly, as the weight of the rope coming down causes the end of the other rope to accelerate, and it may flick higher than the belay and snag. The thought of having to prusik up a precariously snagged rope hardly bears thinking about!

The semi-Dulfer abseil utilizes a sit sling and a karabiner but the ropes pass over the climber's shoulder to gain friction. Very commonly used until recent years, it is only comfortable if the climber's neck and shoulder are well padded. Those vestigial shoulder patches on commando-style pullovers were originally designed to cope with such savage friction.

The most commonly used method of abseiling today uses a Figure 8 friction brake. The climber sits in either harness or sit sling and his rate of descent is easily controlled by increasing the grip of his lower hand, and also varying the angle at which the ropes leave the Figure 8. It is a simple matter to stop and 'lock off' the ropes by taking a number of turns around the device with the main ropes, which can then be clipped back on to themselves with a spare karabiner. Making knots should be avoided since they can easily jam under load.

There are many methods of abseiling; in all methods the climber slides down the rope in a sitting position with his feet pushing against the rock helping to steer some sort of course. Often when passing overhangs, climbers descend great distances without contacting rock. This is called a free abseil.

Six Abseil Methods

Classic method (Dulfer). This barbaric style is no longer used, and a good thing too! However, it should be briefly described. The climber prepares to abseil by standing astride the ropes, passing these under one thigh, across the front of his body and over the opposite shoulder. If the ropes pass over the right shoulder, they are held by the left hand behind the back and vice versa. Braking action is achieved by the friction of the rope against the climber's clothing and, when this is worn through, painfully against his skin!

Modified Dulfer. Though not much of an improvement, this was the standard method of abseiling until very recently, and is still used fairly widely. Here the climber uses a sit sling, often a long tape sling carried for the purpose (and doubling as a runner). A screw gate karabiner is clipped into the sit sling in front of the climber, and the main ropes are led into the karabiner and over either shoulder, to be held by the opposite hand as before. In both the above methods the control hand is the one behind the back, the other hand is used on the ropes in front of the climber simply as a steady; no attempt should be made to gain friction with this hand, since it will merely get hot! If the classic Dulfer method burned the climber at both crotch and shoulder, at least the modified method burns only the shoulder. Climbers who use this method are readily recognized by the streaks of grime ground into their outer garments when abseiling down wet ropes, and one or two who have abseiled in T-shirts can be recognized by the skin grafts on their shoulders!

Figure 8 descender. Many climbers today use a metal friction device to provide a brake. The best known of these is the Clog Figure 8. With this, the ropes are pushed in a bight through the large loop, and are then bent over the top of the small loop so that they pass around the shank. The small loop can then be clipped to the sit sling (or harness) by a screw gate karabiner. From the photographs it can be seen that this device is foolproof, for the ropes cannot be released accidentally. The climber's hands grasp the ropes, one above the brake and the other below. The lower hand is the control, and is easily able to provide more or less friction by varying the angle at which the lower rope leaves the Figure 8, and by increasing grip if greater braking effect is required. The Figure 8 can also be used as a braking aid when belaying, but has not got the same versatility of braking effort as the Sticht plate. It should therefore only be used for bringing up the second man. It is also a heavy and expensive item.

Sticht plate. This versatile piece of equipment will function very well as an abseil brake. It is rigged in the same way as for belaying, the abseil ropes being passed through the plate in a bight and then clipped into the screw karabiner on the climber's harness. Instead of being used to hold the high loads imposed by a falling climber, the

Using a Sticht plate as an abseil brake. As with a Figure 8, the upper hand merely acts as a guide.

Figure 8 Descender. Perhaps the best friction brake for abseiling, It is simple to rig, and its large mass quickly dissipates the great heat generated during an abseil. Its disadvantages are weight and expense.

Rappel Rack. By clipping the ropes through a variable number of bars, the amount of braking can be adjusted. Where fine control is required, this device has its advantages, but has not proved popular with climbers because of its great weight.

Left *Three stages in the assembly of a karabiner brake. A climber intending to use this method is well advised to practice the assembly so that it can be done in adverse conditions without making a mistake.*

1. Two karabiners are held in one hand with their gates on opposite sides, and the bight of the doubled rope is brought upwards through the karabiners in the manner shown. The two (or three) karabiners to be used as brake bars are then clipped through the bight and on around the main ropes.

2. It is then possible to slide the second two krabs back on to the first two . . .

3. . . . and the brake is ready to be clipped to the climber's harness by another karabiner. The assembly is easier if the second pair of karabiners are of fairly large size. If more friction is needed, three krabs can be used as brake bars, and if this isn't enough . . . then . . . (above) *a double assembly should suffice.*

A long, free abseil in the Dolomites. Many climbs in the Alps require lengthy and involved abseils, and a climber must be completely familiar with the technique. A beginner should practice with a safety rope, held from above by a properly belayed companion.

plate is used to brake the relatively gentle loads involved in abseiling. It can't be expected to do both jobs equally well, and when used for abseiling the lower ropes must be constantly fed up towards the plate in order to reduce friction. A word of warning: great heat is generated when abseiling quickly, and those metal braking devices which have a small mass can get very hot indeed. Certainly hot enough to damage the sheath of the rope. It's a good idea therefore, to get into the habit of quickly detaching the ropes from the brake at the bottom of the abseil pitch.

Karabiner brake. This is the favourite method of the expedition mountaineer, because it utilizes equipment he carries anyway, the karabiner, and so saves weight. All braking devices rely on bending the ropes through sharp angles to cause friction. With a karabiner brake, the ropes are fed through a pair of karabiners placed on top of each other with their gates on opposite sides. The doubled abseil ropes can then be fed upwards in a bight through the karabiners. Two other karabiners can be placed under the bights to form brake bars (see photograph). The assembly is then attached to the climber's harness by another karabiner, and the climber is ready to proceed using his lower hand as a control as in other methods.

In practice, various modifications to the assembly of the brake might have to be made. The weight of the climber, thickness of the rope, or the size and shape of the karabiners used, all affect the amount of braking achieved. It may be necessary to use three karabiners as brake bars or even a double assembly to obtain enough friction. Once the right combination has been found, it is a good idea to mark the chosen karabiners with electrical tape so they can be selected without effort when required. It should be remembered that the karabiners must never be rigged so that the ropes can accidentally open the gates. Furthermore, where screw gate karabiners have been used, the ropes running through them should always move in such a way as to screw up the gate—this of course applies to any climbing application.

Rappel rack. This is simply a U-shaped piece of steel rod with a series of aluminium brake bars across it. These can be unclipped at alternate

Opposite:
This climber is abseiling off Bwlch y Moch buttress at Tremadoc in North Wales, rather than walk the half mile round from the top of the crag down to the road. These interesting and popular crags are ancient granite sea cliffs left high and dry by the building of the causeway at Portmadoc.

ends so that the abseil rope might be clipped back in zig-zag fashion without the bother of threading it. Friction is generated around the brake bars. This device does have the virtue of not twisting the ropes, but in its present form is both heavy and expensive. It has more future as a rescue aid, perhaps.

It is worth remembering, that with any method of abseil, it is possible to attach a prusik sling to the main rope, and clip this to the climbing harness. The climber's upper, steadying hand can grasp the prusik knot which will readily slide down the rope as he abseils. In the event of a problem being encountered, his hand releases from the knot which will immediately grip the rope and hold his weight.

Self-Rescue: Prusiking

This is a self-rescue technique whereby a fallen climber, dangling on his main ropes, is able to climb back up the ropes to reach his belay, or at least some piece of terra firma. Most climbers never actually need to prusik, but everyone should have a working knowledge of how it is done. If you are rained off the climbs, an interesting morning can always be spent practising prusik techniques on a large tree or suitable piece of rock. Amongst other things, it will give you a good idea of the type and length of slings you will require to suit a chosen method.

In a climbing incident it is usually best to avoid prusiking if at all possible, since it is both slow and strenuous; often the fallen climber will be able to traverse back on to the climb and so climb back up the rock if it is intended to continue the route. Sometimes it will be more expedient to lower him to a suitable stance where the second can abseil to join him if the party decide that retreat is best, and of course, possible in that direction. Climbing hand over hand up the rope is strictly for Hollywood films and shouldn't be considered.

If the dangling climber is tied on to the main rope by a direct tie around his waist, or a climber's belt, he will want to relieve the suffocating constriction as quickly as possible. This can be done by utilizing the 'baboon hang', first devised in Australia. The climber selects a suitable tape sling and, pivoting on his waist tie, turns upside down. Hooking either leg in front of his main rope, he can then place the tape sling over his feet and work it up his legs until around his upper thighs. With a quick pull up on his main rope, he can sit up with the tape forming a reasonably comfortable sit sling from which he can plan his next moves. Obviously, if he is wearing a harness, all this will not be necessary, but if a tape sling is used in the way described, the length is fairly critical. The climber is now in a position to arrange his prusik slings.

The basic prusik knot is made by wrapping the bight of a sling round the main rope, and threading it through itself at least twice. When pulled tight it has an unmistakeable appearance. The greater the difference in diameter between the main rope and the sling, the more positive is the gripping action of the knot when put under load. However, the small mass of the thinnest slings means there is a real danger of the sling melting when subjected to shock loading. When using 9-mm main ropes, not less than 5-mm prusik slings should be used, and if 11-mm main ropes, 6-mm slings would be better. There are a number of improved prusik knots and some of these are shown in the illustrations on pages 16 to 18. Perhaps the most widely used is the Bachmann knot, which is made around a karabiner, and which offers a welcome handhold. The normal prusik knot is quite satisfactory for emergency use, and it does have the advantage of being able to be tied with one hand.

Two prusik slings are normally used, one for a foot and the other for a chest sling. It is common practice to use quite short slings for the actual prusik knots interlinked with other slings normally used as runners to extend these for use as chest or foot slings. The chest sling should be of tape since the climber's full weight will be on it most of the time. Looking at the diagram, you will see that the relative length of the two prusik slings is important. They should be long enough to extend fully the climber's arms as he pushes the knots up above him, otherwise valuable gain in height will be lost with every upward move.

Progress is made by taking all the weight on each sling alternately, and moving the other sling as high as possible as the weight is taken off it. Having his weight supported high up by a chest sling means less strain on the climber's arms when keeping himself upright; by the same token, it is helpful if the foot sling passes under the chest sling to gain some support from it. The most difficult part is starting off, but after climbing a few feet the going becomes definitely easier, if strenuous. Five feet per minute could be considered a good rate of progress.

Meanwhile the belayed climber might be in a

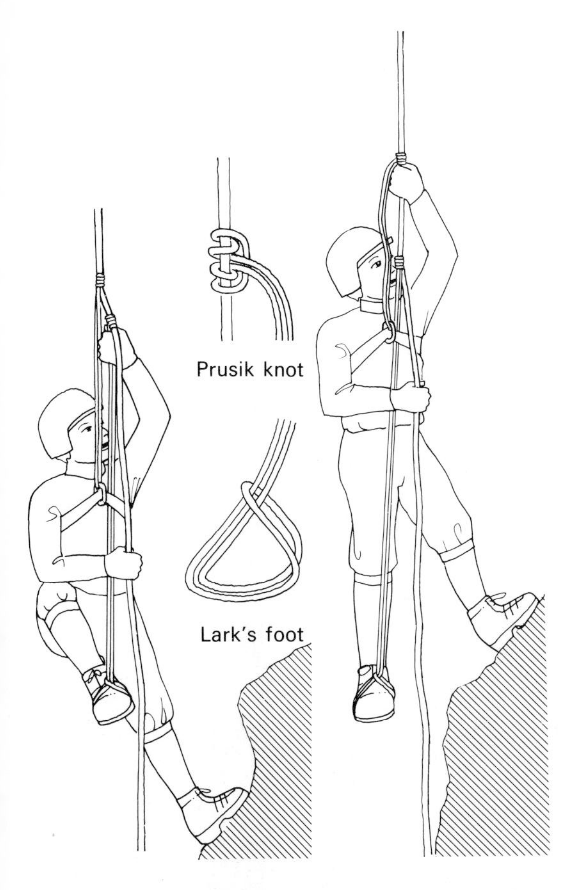

The Prusiking Sequence. *There are two slings in use, a chest sling and a foot sling; it is important that the chest sling is broad and comfortable because the climber's full weight is on it all the time. Here, therefore, it has been shown as a tape sling linked to the actual prusik sling by a karabiner. It is impractical to use a long tape as a prusik since the tape will not grip. Note that the foot sling passes inside the chest sling. It is better if the climber slips his foot into a loop (lark's foot) in the foot sling. Either hand can be used to push the knots up, and either foot can be in the sling. The free foot is used to push off the rock, and the free hand must be used to hold the main rope down when the knots are moved up. Prusiking in this way is quite straightforward. The climber merely hangs from the chest sling while moving the knot on the foot sling as high as possible; he can then stand up on the foot sling sliding up the chest sling as he does so. It is a strenuous operation, and one which requires some practice before the day when you might have to do it for real!*

position to offer help. He should attempt to secure the main rope as soon as communication has been established with his fallen partner. Depending on his method of belay, this will be more or less awkward, but he must put a prusik sling on the loaded rope whilst still holding his partners' weight with his control hand, and clip this prusik sling directly onto the belay anchor with a karabiner. Having achieved this, he can lower the loaded rope onto the prusik knot, watching it carefully to ensure that it is not likely to slip. He is now in a position to make fast the loaded rope to the anchor point using a figure eight knot and screw karabiner.

If double ropes are being used, the fallen climber uses one of them to prusik up, while the second safeguards him, taking as much of his weight as he can on the second rope. This can be a considerable help, and a good reason for climbing on double ropes. (Another method depends on the belayer fixing prusik slings on both ropes from the anchor point and taking in each rope alternately as his partner transfers his weight from rope to rope, usually using two foot slings. This idea, though good, is really too sophisticated for any but the most expert.)

Where the climbers are using single 11-mm rope, it is more difficult for the belayer to give help, depending on the amount of rope available at the belay. If the man on the belay estimates that he has sufficient rope to reach his fallen partner there's nothing to stop him from untying from the main rope (after first securing himself to the belay by slings), and lowering the end to his partner to give him assistance as before. It is even possible to improve his pulling power by lowering a karabiner on a bight of rope and thus obtaining a two to one purchase. However, if the fall has been a long one, with a single rope the belayer might be able to offer no assistance at all, since the rope end might not reach anywhere near his partner.

The best answer, then, is for each climber to be certain that he can prusik for long distances unaided—and that means practice.

Prusiking has become important enough in modern mountaineering for a number of mechanical prusikers, or ascenders as they are known, to have been specially designed for the purpose. On many of the world's biggest climbs, only one climber actually climbs the rock, the rest of the party climb the ropes. These climbs are so arduous and time consuming that often two pairs

Left *Clogwyn Climbing gear 'Expedition' ascender, a mechanical prusiking device much used on big wall climbs. The toothed cam grips the rope for climbing yet is able to slide easily up the rope as required. A safety catch above the climber's thumb prevents accidental removal of the ascender from the rope.*

Centre *Gibbs Ascender. The fastest prusiking device, and the most effective on icy ropes. Its one drawback is that it can't be attached to the rope with one hand. The cast alloy cam is detached by pulling out the quick release pin, after which the rope can be put into the housing and the cam replaced.*

Right *This is the famous Swiss made Jumar clamp, the original mechanical prusiking device. The action of the cam is clearly seen; below the cam a plastic trigger prevents accidental disengagement. The jumar is made from cast aluminium, and fracturing of the frame has caused some incidents. Because of this danger it is now customary to reinforce the handle with nylon tape fastened between the top lug and the foot sling. The nylon tape is itself bound to the handle with electrical tape to keep the job neat.*

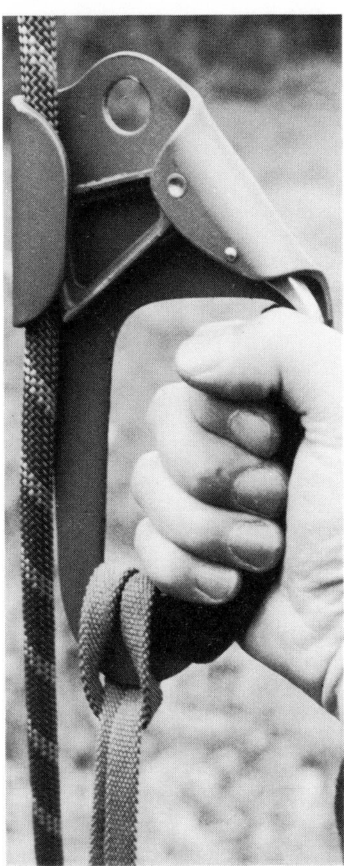

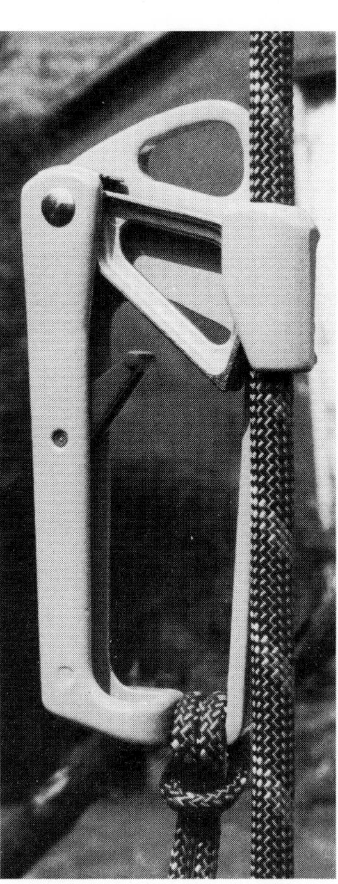

of climbers climb together, alternating leads on different days. The pair not leading spend their time in hauling the whole party's food and equipment. Mechanical devices are essential for this type of climbing, being very much faster than using knots. Indeed the Gibbs ascender is credited with a record of a hundred feet climbed in just 39 seconds!

Guide Books and Grading

A rock climbing guide is primarily intended to record details of routes climbed, and to give indications of length, seriousness and grade of those climbs. Rock climbs usually follow natural features, be they gullies, cracks, or ridges. A climb should follow an independent line, and have a distinct character. When a route is first climbed, the first ascent party record the details in a 'new

Clogwyn y Grochan, a typical British crag, and one of half a dozen to be found in the Llanberis Pass in Snowdonia. It has about forty climbs, mostly around the Very Severe standard, a grade which most people will be capable of seconding by the end of their first season's climbing.

A climber in some trouble: he is following the final pitch of Dream of White Horses, Hard VS, on Craig Gogarth. It is a very windy day and occasionally sheets of spray are blown right up the cliff from the sea over a hundred feet below. The updraught is so strong that some of the runners put on by the leader have blown off. The second was eventually extricated by the leader hauling through one of the two ropes and dropping it to his partner from directly above him, weighted with a large stone. When the second had tied on, the leader was able to protect him on this rope from above while the difficult traverse to the left was made.

route' book (often found at a club hut), the climb is subsequently checked by the writer of the guide, and the details are eventually published.

A single guide might cover only climbs on a particular crag or perhaps several crags in one area. Usually it will contain details of a hundred climbs or more, and there are usually brief notes on the history of climbing in the area. Flora and fauna and geology might also be covered.

It is the privilege of the first ascent party to name the climb, and the naming of routes is a subject in itself. From the intricate Kipling Groove (Ruddy'ard), the mystical Dream of White Horses the alliterative Shrike and the devious Tapes Last Krapp, we can gain some insight into the times and the characters of the originators.

If a first ascent party walk up to the foot of an unclimbed line, put on the ropes and climb the route, they are said to have made an 'on sight' first ascent. Regrettably, competition for new climbs combined with the sheer difficulty of modern high standard rock climbing has made onsight first ascents an increasingly rare occurrence. There are various ways of making a new route easier to climb for the first time; these range from 'gardening' grass and loose rock, often from abseil, to 'practising moves', where the climber abseils to the supposed difficult sections of the new climb and repeatedly attempts the crux until he succeeds in climbing it, meanwhile protected by a rope from above. It is not unknown for protection runners to be pre-placed at this stage, so that the leader merely has to clip his ropes in when first making the climb. There is a certain amount of unscrupulousness in this, since there is no doubt that these climbs, difficult though they may be, are capable of being climbed without dubious tactics being employed when a good enough climber comes along, though admittedly, this might take a matter of years rather than months.

Grading

If the definition of a camel is a horse designed by a committee, then one could be excused for thinking that the selfsame committee was responsible for the methods of grading rock climbs! The idea of giving a grade to a route is, of course, to warn the unwary that a climb might be more difficult and hence more dangerous than it appears.

It is easy with hindsight to see where the early grading systems went wrong. By the end of the Edwardian era, the grades Easy, Moderately Difficult, Difficult, Very Difficult and Severe had been applied to climbs. Before 1920 the grade Very Severe was introduced; after this there was an interval of thirty years before a harder grade was awarded to a climb. It would be inconceivable to suppose that standards of climbing had not risen, and in fact they had increased enormously. What had happened was that there had been a marked reluctance to adopt a grade with a title more superlative than Very Severe. How *could* any climb be harder than Very Severe? This conservative attitude resulted in many new climbs being graded VS when, in fact, they were a good deal harder than others of the same grade climbed many years before. The result was a considerable spectrum of difficulty in the VS grade.

After 1950, there came a spate of new routes, apparently so horrendous, that new grades simply had to be found. The grades Hard VS, Extremely Severe and Exceptionally Severe were quickly introduced (at least in Wales). The Exceptionally Severe grading was the first attempt to bring in that particular intangible—seriousness—into the grade of a climb. In rock climbing, seriousness means risk, and is associated with exposure, loose rock, poor protection, etc. It was subsequently withdrawn, and for the next ten years or so Extreme held the crown for the hardest grade in much the same way as Very Severe had twenty years before; and yet more hard routes than ever were being made. In 1977 the sensible course was at last taken, the Extreme grade was sub-divided into five grades at a stroke, E1 to E5, obviously for tomorrow's supermen it is simply necessary to add to the numbers!

It is becoming increasingly common, at least in Wales and the Lake District guides, to grade individual pitches. Some critics say that, together with too fulsome route descriptions, this takes some of the sense of discovery from a climb. To pick a recent example the climb Rat Race on Craig

Comparative table of international grading systems.

BRITISH ADJECTIVAL	BRITISH * PITCH GRADE	UIAA	AMERICAN DECIMAL	FRENCH	GERMAN	AUSTRALIAN
easy		I	1	facile	leïcht	
			2			
moderately difficult		II	3	peu facile	massig schwerig	
difficult		III– III III+	4 5·0 5·1	assez difficile (AD)	zïemlich schwerig	
very difficult severe	4a	IV– IV IV+	5·2 5·3 5·4	difficile (D Sup.) difficile supérieur	schwerig	12 13
						14
hard severe very severe hard very severe	4b 4c	V– V V+	5·5 5·6 5·7	très Difficile inférieur très difficile (TD) très difficile supérieur (TD Sup.)	sehr schwerig	15 16 17 18
E1 mild extreme	5a	VI–	5·8	extremement difficile (ED)	ausserzt schwerig	19 20
E2	5b	VI	5·9			21
E3 extreme	5c	VI+	5·10 a,b,c,d			22 23
E4	6a		5·11 a,b,c,d			
E5 hard extreme	6b		5·12 a,b,c,d			

*Comparison of International Grading. Pitch grading refers to technical difficulty; overall grade gives indication of seriousness, i.e. a route with two 5c pitches would probably carry a grade E4.

Opposite:
Yosemite granite, young rock with clean and definite features. This climb is Phoenix, graded 5.12b, the hardest rock climb in the Valley—for the moment at any rate. The climber is Ray Jardine. Yosemite became famous for the quality of its Big Wall climbs, particularly on the 3000-foot buttresses of El Capitan where there are a number of multi-day routes (photo: George Mayers).

Gogarth carries an overall grading of XS E2 and has five pitches individually graded 5a, 5c, 5a, 4c, 5a. So obviously, together with the detailed written description, the aspiring leader has a good foreknowledge of the climb. Pitch gradings are the subject of a great deal of debate among climbers, who enjoy the subject immensely.

Reference to the comparative diagram will show other systems of grading, and how they compare with the British one. In France and in the other Continental climbing countries, there is a similar situation to that of the UK. Until just recently, the top grade of ED+ in France and 6+ in the other countries had been regarded as finite. It is surely little short of arrogance, on the part of the climbing Establishment of these countries (who control the grading systems), that the hardest routes of their own generation are the most difficult that can be humanly achieved! There is some sign of revolt with some recent climbs being graded 7 by their originators—though not ratified yet by their national authorities.

In the United States, a decimal system of grading is used. This included various grades of walking and scrambling; all rock climbing was intended to be in the fifth grade with subdivisions based on a decimal. Thus, if 5·1 was the easiest of rock climbs, then 5·9 would be the hardest. As elsewhere, American climbers got better and better, and the grades were simply extended to 5·10, then 5·11and now 5·12—perhaps illogical, but certainly effective. Even more subtle subdivisions have recently been added to 5·10 and above, denoted by a, b, c, d.

Rock climbing is a young sport in Australia. The pioneers observed the paradoxes evident in other people's grading systems before adopting their own. From the start they used open-ended grades, thus grade 19 is equivalent to British E1, 22 equivalent to E3 and so on. What a nice simple system!

Very steep rock can be climbed using artificial techniques, indeed some of the bigger 'roofs' climbed measure 200 feet across. This climb, the Main Overhang on Malham Cove in Yorkshire, goes straight over the large roof on expansion bolts; it is graded A1. The climber is Tut Braithwaite.

Equipment Check List

Camping can be the answer if you want to go on extended climbing trips. Modern tents come in all shapes and sizes, but the following will give you an idea of where to begin.

Modern tents are both lightweight and windcheating; with this type, hoops of glass fibre ensure stability when the tent is pitched and make the most of the space inside. Although a lightweight design is very desirable if mountain camping is contemplated, many climbers habitually camp close to their vehicles, and are better off with one of the larger, cheaper cotton tents which are available.

Vango Mk. 3 Std.; a popular tent with climbers for many years, it has a cotton inner tent and flysheet which arrangement is less likely to give condensation problems. The weight of this type makes it less suitable for high mountain camping than some others.

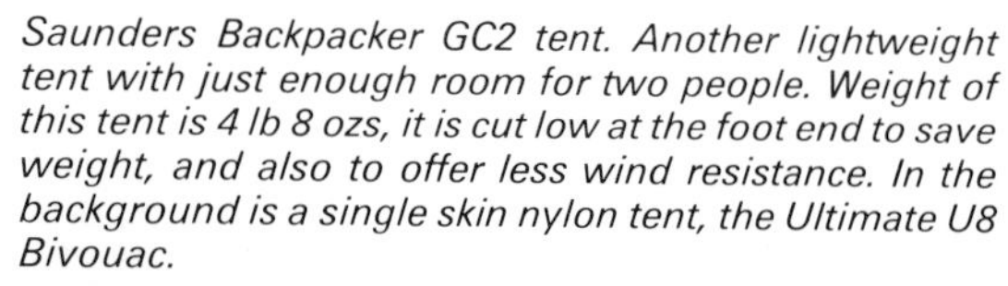

Saunders Backpacker GC2 tent. Another lightweight tent with just enough room for two people. Weight of this tent is 4 lb 8 ozs, it is cut low at the foot end to save weight, and also to offer less wind resistance. In the background is a single skin nylon tent, the Ultimate U8 Bivouac.

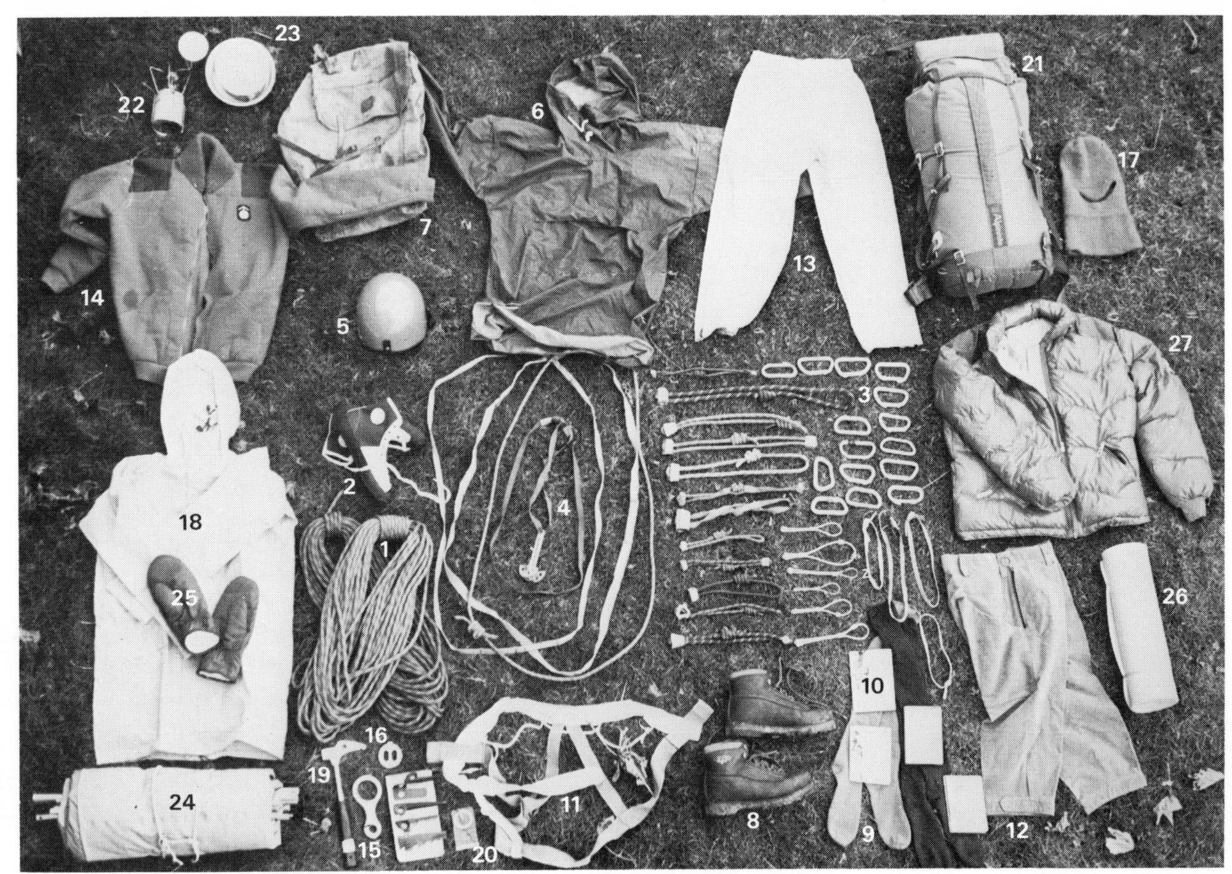

One climber's paraphernalia. Generally speaking, the more important items are listed first, though some people would disagree with the sequence. A sleeping bag could have been included, particularly since many climbers camp. The first half-dozen items will start you climbing; the rest can follow later.

1. *Two 9-mm ropes, 45 m in length (Edelweiss Extrem).*
2. *Rock boots (EB's).*
3. *A variety of nut slings (some wired) and 15 karabiners. The four short tape slings are for use with the wired nuts.*
4. *Three long slings, of which two are tape, and one rope. There is also a shorter tape sling with a 'Friend' in the middle.*
5. *Climbing helmet (JB lightweight).*
6. *Lightweight neoprene-proofed cagoule.*
7. *Daysack, rather an old one but a good 'un (BB Snowcap).*
8. *Mountain boots. Comfortable and dependable, but not the best I've ever climbed in (La Dolomite K2).*
9. *Two pairs of stockings.*
10. *Rock climbing guides.*
11. *Whillans sit harness (Troll Products).*
12. *Breeches: these are brushed mole cord (JB Hoyle).*
13. *Waterproof overtrousers: 4-oz neoprene Thor, with side zips so you can get them on without removing your boots.*
14. *North Cape polar jacket, model 'Ogre'.*
15. *Figure 8 Descender.*
16. *Sticht Plate, with spring.*
17. *Brushed wool balaclava, worth its weight in gold on a bad day in the mountains.*
18. *Henri-Lloyd Glencoe jacket; an 8-oz, neoprene-proofed, zipped jacket. Probably the best on the market for wet weather walking, but rather heavy for rock climbing.*
19. *Peg hammer and, of course, a few pegs.*
20. *Map and compass for hardy mountain walkers.*
21. *Alpine climbing sack. An expensive item which should only be bought after careful thought (Karrimor Haston Alpiniste).*
22. *Gaz stove. A number of lightweight designs are available, the alternative stoves, run on petrol or paraffin are much more expensive.*
23. *Cooking utensils*
24. *Tent, again a bewildering variety can be bought; usually the ultra-lightweight types sacrifice durability for weight, and are expensive.*
25. *Mitts, really a mountain walking item.*
26. *Insulating mat of closed cell foam. Indispensable to the camper and also to the Alpine climber.*
27. *Duvet jacket. A necessity only for colder Alpine routes. Synthetic fillings have reduced the price of these garments in recent years.*

Climbing Areas and Associations

UNITED KINGDOM

In the UK the central representative body for mountaineers and rock climbers is the

British Mountaineering Council
Precinct Centre
Booth Street East

You can become an individual member, but most local clubs are affiliated to the BMC.

The main climbing areas are as follows:

South England Harrisons Rocks, Tunbridge Wells; Swanage sea cliffs; Cornwall sea cliffs; Lundy Island sea cliffs; Cheddar Gorge; Avon Gorge.
Derbyshire Stoney Middleton.
Sheffield area Stanage; Froggat, Curbar Edges.
South Wales Gower sea cliffs; Pembroke sea cliffs.
Mid Wales Dolgellau area.
North Wales Ogwen Valley; Llanberis Pass; Clogwyn D'ur Arddu; Gogarth sea cliff.
Yorkshire Almscliffe; Malham Cove.
Lake District Borrowdale; Scafell; Langdale.
Northumberland Cleveland outcrops.
Scotland Arran; Arrochar; Glencoe; Ben Nevis; Skye; Cairngorms; Torridon; Orkney sea cliffs.
Northern Ireland Fair Head sea cliffs; Mourne mountains.

EIRE

Federation of Mountain Clubs of Ireland
Sorbonne 7
Ardilea Estate
Dublin 14

Areas: Wicklow Mountains; Donegal.

USA

American Alpine Club
113 East 90th Street
New York
NY 10028

Areas: Shawangunks, New York State; Yosemite National Park, California; Eldorado Canyon, Arizona; Boulder, Colorado; Tetons, New Mexico.

CANADA

Alpine Club of Canada
PO Box 1026
Baff-Alta
and
Fédération Quebeçoise de la Montagne
1415 East Jarry Street
Montreal
Quebec HZE 2Z7

Areas: Bugaboos, Rockies, British Columbia; Squamish Chief, Vancouver; Calgary.

AUSTRALIA AND NEW ZEALAND

Areas: Frog Buttress, Queensland; Mount Maroon, Queensland; Warrumbungles, New South Wales; Blue Mountains, NSW; Ball's Pyramid (sea stack 1800 feet), NSW; Mount Arapiles; Victoria; Buffalo Gorge, Victoria; Frenchman's Cap, Tasmania; Darrang Ranges, South Island, NZ.

SOUTH AFRICA AND KENYA

Areas: Table Mountain; Drakensburg; Hell's Gate Gorge; Mount Kenya.

FRANCE

Fédération Française de la Montagne
7 rue de la Boetie
75008 Paris

Areas: Mt Blanc massif; Dauphine; gorges of the Vercors and Verdon Gorge; Alpes maritimes; Fontainbleau outcrops; Calanques sea cliffs.

Yosemite Valley is the main centre for climbing in the Sierra Nevada Mountains.

SWITZERLAND

Schweizer Alpen Club
Geschäftsstelle SAC
Helvetiaplatz 4
3005 Bern
and
Club Suisse de Femmes Alpinistes
Balderngasse 9
8001 Zürich

Areas: Numerous, mostly with some ice.

ITALY

Club alpino Italiano
Via Ugo Foscolo 3
20121 Milano
or
Federazione Italiana Sport Invernali
Via Cerva 30
20122 Milano

Areas: Dolomites; Courmayeur.

AUSTRIA

Verband Alpiner Vereine Österreichs
Bäckerstrasse 16 (II)
1010 Wien 1
or
Osterreichischer Alpenverein
Wilhelm-Greil-Strasse 15
6010 Innsbruck

Areas: Dachstein; Kaisergebirge; Wetterstein; Stubaital.

WEST GERMANY

Deutscher Alpenverein
Praterinsel 5
8 München 22

Areas: Black Forest area; Harz Mountains; Karwendel, Bavaria.

NORWAY

Norsk Tindeklub
Post Boks 1727
Vika
Oslo 1

Areas: Romsdal Valley; Andalsnes; Lofoten Islands.

BELGIUM

Club Alpin Belge
Rue de l'Aurore 19
1050 Bruxelles

Areas: Ardennes, particularly Freyr.

Organizations and Clubs

Accrington Caper Montis Mountaineering Club
Hon. Sec. D. J. Ormerod
184 Richmond Road
Accrington

Avon Mountaineering Club
Sec. Dave Taylor
1 The Elms
Malmains Drive
Bristol BS16 1PZ

Banbury Mountaineering Club
c/o Reindeer Inn
Parsons Street
Banbury

Barrow Mountaineering and Ski Club
Sec. J. Garstang
Overbeck
Penny Bridge
Ulverston
Cumbria

Birmingham Carabiner Club
Sec. Val Comery
206 Perry Wood Road
Birmingham B42 2BH

Braintree Outdoor Pursuits Club
Gen. Sec. R. Hawkins
30 Chestnut Avenue
Gosfield, Halstead
Essex

Brathay Exploration Group
Expeditions Sec.
Old Brathay
Ambleside
Cumbria LA22 0HN

Carlisle Mountaineering Club
Hut Sec. M. Miller
The Haven
Thornthwaite
Keswick

Castle Mountaineering Club (Scotland)
Hon. Sec. Alec Barclay
32 Pentland Park
Livingston
West Lothian

Cave & Crag Club (Birmingham)
Hon. Sec. D. Snell
Comberford
Tamworth

Ceunant Mountaineering Club (Birmingham)
Sec. Mrs P. Rooker
23 Neville Road
Erdington
Birmingham

Chester Mountaineering Club
Marian Mitchell
7 Cecil Street
Boughton
Chester

Clwyd Mountaineering Club
Richard Owen
55 Rhuddlan Road
Rhyl
Clwyd

Coventry Mountaineering Club
Sec. H. Calvert
99 Aldbury Rise
Allesley Park
Coventry

Croydon Mountaineering Club
Bernard Ingrams
10 Kerrill Avenue
Old Coulsdon
Surrey

Cym Cywarch
P. George
15 Berkeley Close
Alders Green
Redditch B98 0QB

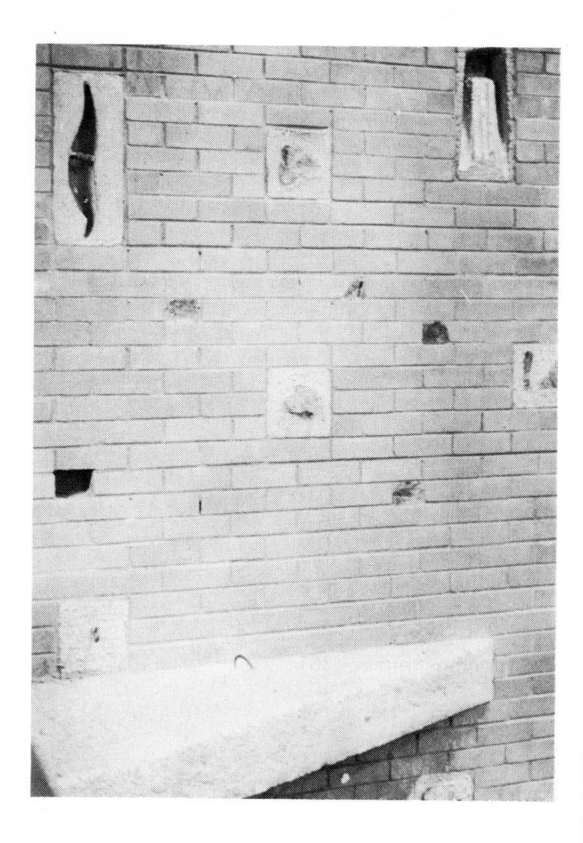

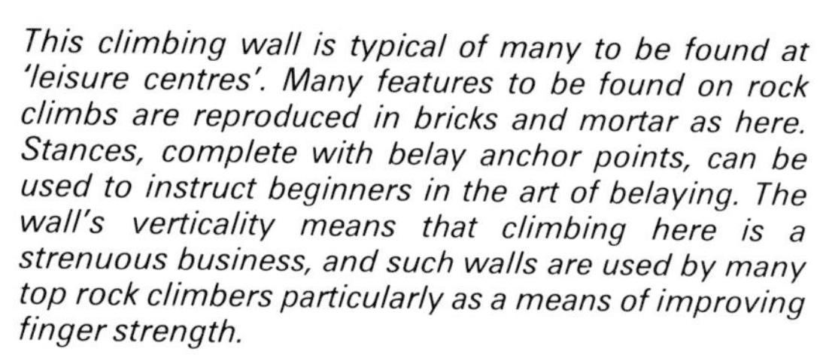

This climbing wall is typical of many to be found at 'leisure centres'. Many features to be found on rock climbs are reproduced in bricks and mortar as here. Stances, complete with belay anchor points, can be used to instruct beginners in the art of belaying. The wall's verticality means that climbing here is a strenuous business, and such walls are used by many top rock climbers particularly as a means of improving finger strength.

Derby Mountaineering Club
Sec. Ron Langlois
14 Leven Close
Sinfin
Derby DE2 3HP

Doncaster Mountaineering Club
Sec. Andy Brocklesby
22 Wentworth Close
Whitley Bridge

East Yorkshire Mountaineering Club
Sec. Geoff Haigh
22 Barry House
Bransholme
Hull
East Yorks

Gentain Club
Sec. George Watkins
'Hollandia'
Butterrow West
Rodborough
Stroud
Glos

Gloucestershire Mountaineering Club
Sec. Mrs S. Foord
1 Pixiefields
Cradley
Malvern
Worcs

Grimsby Mountaineering Club
Ernie Gawthrop
Tel. Grimsby 813702

Gwent Mountaineering Club
Trefor Beese
8 Glade Close
Coedeva
Cwmbran
Gwent

Gwydyr Mountain Club
Hon. Sec. Les Fowles
89 Arrowe Park Road
Upton
Wirral
Merseyside

Hampshire Mountaineering Association
Sec. Barbara Humberstone
20 Randall Close
Calmore
Southampton

Hereford Mountain Club
Sec. Ralph Goddard
37 Bodenham Road
Hereford

Hertfordshire Mountaineering Club
Sec. D. J. Goodey
4 Tenison Avenue
Boreham Wood
Herts

Irish Mountaineering Club
Hon. Sec.
183 Clonkeen Crescent
Pottery Road
Dunlaoghaire

Jacobites' Mountaineering Club (Edinburgh)
Sec. Dr Martin Plant
18 Morningside Gardens
Edinburgh EH10 5LE

J.M.C.S. Edinburgh
Hon. Sec. P. W. Myles
59 Morningside Park
Edinburgh EH10 5EZ

Lancashire Climbing Club
R. Hampson
80 Mill Lane
Coppull
Nr. Chorley PR7 5AN

Lancaster Mountaineering Club
John Wadeson
133 Scotforth Road
Lancaster

Lands End Climbing Club
Janet Atherton
7 Parc-an-Gate
Mousehole
Penzance

Leeds Outdoor Pursuits Club
Sec. Dick Sewell
Tel. Leeds 649441

Liverpool Mountaineering Club
Sec. M. R. Trott
59 South Barcombe Road
Childwall
Liverpool L16 7QE

Lomond Mountaineering Club (Glasgow)
Sec. George Christie
147 Drumoyne Road
Glasgow G51 4BA

Macclesfield Mountaineering Club
Sec. Alan Jackson
Tel. Macclesfield 612361

Maidstone Mountaineering Club
Sec. Tom Phillips
12 Ashford Road
Maidstone
Kent

Manchester Mountaineering Club
Sec. Dave Croker
14 Milwain Road
Stretford
Manchester

Marylebone Mountaineering Club (London)
65 Gondar Gardens
London NW6

Mercian Mountaineering Club
Sec. B. A. Carter
12 Roundmoor Walk
Castle Vale
Birmingham

Northumbrian Mountaineering Club
Sec. J. W. Earl
13 East Acres
Dinnington
Newcastle-upon-Tyne N13 7NA

Nottingham Rock and Heather Club
Secretary
Cherry House Club
9 Redhill Road
Arnold
Nottingham

Ochils Mountaineering Club
Secretary
The Square
Gargunnock
Stirling

Oxford Mountaineering Club
Hon. Sec. Mike Dunn
16 Salisbury Crescent
Oxford

Reading Mountaineering Club
Sec. Pete Sutton
17 Mill Lane
Earley
Reading

Rosyth Civil Service Mountaineering Club
Sec. J. Fernie
42 Garnock Terrace
Dunfermline

Rutland Mountaineering Club
Secretary
197a Enderby Road
Whetstone
Leicester

Shropshire Mountaineering Club
Sec. G. Watkins
Flat 9
90 Haygate Road
Telford
Salop

Slough Mountaineering Club
Sec. Jane Sellwood
Shinfield Lodge
Church Lane
3-mile Cross
Reading

South Cheshire Climbing Club
Sec. Dave Mason
49 Park Estate
Shavington
Crewe

A long run out, the first pitch of a classic British rock climb, Great Slab on Cloggy (Clogwyn D'ur Arddu). The leader has climbed about a hundred feet, and has a further forty to climb to reach a belay. Leads of this length are common enough, but it's as well to remember that it's the height of a 15-storey building. Welsh names are not always what they seem. There is a climb on Cloggy for instance, whose name Naddyn Ddu when properly pronounced is the Yorkshiremans traditional greeting 'Na then thee!'. The first ascent was made by a Sheffield team.

South Devon Mountaineering Club
Sec. Ron King
6 Marine Parade
Dawlish

South Essex Climbing Club
Sec. Les Hodson
164 Severn Drive
Upminster

South Glamorgan Mountaineering Assoc.
Sec. Graham West
16 St Paul's Avenue
Barry
South Glamorgan

South Wales Mountaineering Club
Secretary
S.W.M.C.
Birchgrove Hotel
Caerphilly Road
Cardiff

South Yorkshire Mountaineering Club
Secretary
Hoylands Sports Centre
West Street
Hoyland
Barnsley

St Helens Mountaineering Club
Sec. A. M. Wallace
28 Cecil Street
Sutton
St Helens

Swaledale Outdoor Club
Sec. John Deighton
60 Silver Street
Barton
Richmond
North Yorkshire

Swindon Mountaineering Club
Sec. Gill Allport
11 Ashwell Close
Swindon

The Deaf Mountaineering Club
Sec. Colin Macdonald
58 Brownhill Road
Glasgow

The Mountain Club, Stafford
Sec. J. Hall
37 Wolverhampton Road
Stafford ST17 4DA

Thurrock Mountaineering Assoc.
Sec. F. Broughton
Tel. Hornchurch 54176

Tuesday Climbing Club
Sec. Martin Walker
33 Eagle Lane
London E11 1PF

Vibram Mountaineering Club
Hon. Sec. Charles Joynson
11 South Croft Gate
Bradford BD11 2DQ

Wanneys Climbing Club
Sec. Michael Chapman
91 Rothwell Road
Newcastle-upon-Tyne NE3 1UA

Wellingborough Mountaineering Club
Hon. Sec. Harriet Faulkner
Ten Smith Close
Piddington
Northampton

Wessex Mountaineering Club
Sec. Dave Lankshear
94 Coburg Road
Dorchester
Dorset DT1 2HR

Wigan Rambling and Climbing Club
Sec. Barbara Lane
1 Morden Avenue
Ashton-in-Makerfield
Wigan

Yeti Club
Sec. Brian Taylor
46 Bury Holme
Wormley
Herts
or John Henson
65 Montrose Avenue
Lillington
Leamington Spa
Warks